Digital-Age Literacy for Teachers

Applying Technology Standards to Everyday Practice

Susan Brooks-Young

International Society for Technology in Education
EUGENE, OREGON • WASHINGTON, DC

Digital-Age Literacy for Teachers

Applying Technology Standards to Everyday Practice

Susan Brooks-Young

ACQUISITIONS EDITOR
Scott Harter

PRODUCTION EDITOR
Lynda Gansel

GRAPHIC DESIGNER
Signe Landin

PRODUCTION COORDINATOR
Maddelyn High

RIGHTS AND PERMISSIONS ADMINISTRATOR
Diane Durrett

COPY EDITOR
Nancy Olson

COVER AND BOOK DESIGN
Kim McGovern

LAYOUT AND PRODUCTION
Kim McGovern

First Edition
ISBN: 978-1-56484-229-9

Printed in the United States of America

International Society for Technology in Education (ISTE)
Washington, DC, Office:
1710 Rhode Island Ave. NW, Suite 900, Washington, DC 20036

Eugene, Oregon, Office:
180 West 8th Ave., Suite 300, Eugene, OR 97401-2916

Order Desk: 1.800.336.5191
Order Fax: 1.541.302.3778
Customer Service: orders@iste.org
Book Publishing: books@iste.org
Rights and Permissions: permissions@iste.org
Book Sales and Marketing: booksmarketing@iste.org
Web: www.iste.org

About ISTE

The International Society for Technology in Education (ISTE) is the trusted source for professional development, knowledge generation, advocacy, and leadership for innovation. ISTE is the premier membership association for educators and education leaders engaged in improving teaching and learning by advancing the effective use of technology in PK–12 and teacher education.

Home of the National Educational Technology Standards (NETS) and ISTE's annual conference and exposition (formerly known as NECC), ISTE represents more than 100,000 professionals worldwide. We support our members with information, networking opportunities, and guidance as they face the challenge of transforming education. To find out more about these and other ISTE initiatives, visit our website at **www.iste.org**.

As part of our mission, ISTE Book Publishing works with experienced educators to develop and produce practical resources for classroom teachers, teacher educators, and technology leaders. Every manuscript we select for publication is carefully peer-reviewed and professionally edited. We value your feedback on this book and other ISTE products. E-mail us at **books@iste.org**.

About the Author

Susan Brooks-Young has been involved in instructional technology since 1979. She was one of the first teachers in her district to use technology in the classroom and has continued to explore ways it can be used for student learning. She has worked as a computer mentor, technology trainer, and technology curriculum specialist. As a site administrator, she continued to place a high priority on technology and in 1993 founded Computer Using Educators' (CUE) Administrators Special Interest Group, which still serves as a network and resource for school administrators in the United States and Canada.

Before establishing her own consulting firm, Susan was a teacher, site administrator, and technology specialist at a county office of education, a career that spanned more than 23 years. She now works with school districts and regional centers on technology-related issues, develops curriculum, presents workshops, teaches online courses, and writes articles for a variety of education journals.

Susan co-chairs ISTE's Special Interest Group for Administrators. She has also authored several popular books for school administrators who want to ensure that students and teachers can take full advantage of the unique capabilities of technology in the classroom.

Acknowledgment

Many thanks to Ryan Imbriale, e-learning specialist for Baltimore County Public Schools, Office of Instructional Technology, for his comments, questions, and suggestions throughout the writing of this book.

Other ISTE Titles by the Author

Making Technology Standards Work for You: A Guide for School Administrators, and its companion book, *Self-Assessment Activities for School Administrators*

The Electronic Briefcase for Administrators: Tools and Templates

101 Best Web Sites for District Leaders

101 Best Web Sites for Principals

Contents

Introduction

It is a terrible thing to see and have no vision.
—HELEN KELLER
(attributed by D. Kenny; CEO, National Institute for the Blind of Ireland; 2006)

The quotation above encapsulates the dilemma educators face today when it comes to the role of technology in schools. The dilemma is that since the 1980s, we've seen rapid advances in technology development that have significantly impacted nearly every facet of American life *except* life in the classroom. Desktop computers appeared in K–12 classrooms approximately 25 years ago, and early adopters of instructional technology were certain that computers would redefine education practice in the United States. We now know that this belief was optimistic. Why? The necessary vision has been missing.

Try to imagine everyday life outside of school without a laptop, cell phone, personal digital assistant, digital camera, DVD player, MP3 player, or any one of a number of other technologies that were rare or nonexistent 25 years ago. Imagine not being able to access the Internet using a high-speed connection. Now think about your classroom. How many of these technologies are readily available to you and your students? If your situation is like that of many educators, you can relate to the student who said, "When I get to school, I feel like I have to power down before I go inside."

A primary reason for this situation is the fact that technology integration requires a coherent vision for systemic reform, a vision that must be supported by the entire educational community. In fact, systemic reform is so critical that the International Society for Technology in Education (ISTE) has identified 10 elements, or "Essential Conditions," that must be in place, stating that in the absence of these Essential Conditions teachers cannot be expected to incorporate technology use as an integral part of the teaching and learning process. These Essential Conditions are shown in table 0.1.

Unfortunately, the reality is that many teachers and administrators don't have the necessary background in either system change or technology integration to implement and sustain reform. The purpose of the National Educational Technology Standards for Teachers (NETS•T) is to provide guidelines to assist in addressing the Essential Conditions as you work to implement effective use of technology as a tool for teaching and learning.

TABLE 0.1 ■ **Essential Conditions for effective technology integration**

Shared Vision	There is proactive leadership and administrative support from the entire system.
Access	Educators have access to current technologies, software, and telecommunications networks.
Skilled Educators	Educators are skilled in the use of technology for learning.
Professional Development	Educators have consistent access to professional development in support of technology use in teaching and learning.
Technical Assistance	Educators have technical assistance for maintaining and using the technology.
Content Standards and Curriculum Resources	Educators are knowledgeable in their subject matter and current in the content standards and teaching methodologies in their discipline.
Student-Centered Teaching	Teaching in all settings encompasses student-centered approaches to learning.
Assessment	There is continuous assessment of the effectiveness of technology for learning.
Community Support	The community and school partners provide expertise, support, and resources.
Support Policies	School and university policies, financing, and rewards structures are in place to support technology in learning.

The term *information superhighway* was coined as early as 1991 and reflected the high degree of national interest in getting onto the World Wide Web. Within 2 years, the first edition of the NETS•T, which included 13 performance indicators, was released. Four years later, the second edition of the NETS•T, consisting of 18 performance indicators grouped into three categories, was adopted. Then, in 2000, the NETS•T third edition, modeled on the National Educational Technology Standards for Students (NETS•S) was released. Three editions in the course of 7 years may seem excessive; however, each NETS•T edition reflects the rapidly changing landscape of technology and the increased understanding of the teacher's role in the successful use of technology as a classroom tool.

Another shift has occurred since the most recent revision of these standards. The NETS•T were originally developed with the preservice teacher in mind. Today, we understand that all teachers, regardless of how many years have been spent in the classroom, must be held accountable for at least basic mastery of the performance indicators for the NETS•T. Therefore, it's not unusual today to find that professional development trainings, continuing education courses, and other learning opportunities for experienced teachers are now aligned with the NETS•T. But short-term workshops and classes aren't enough. Teachers need to reexamine their approach to instruction and develop long-range plans for making change.

The purpose of this book is to be a tool for both preservice and experienced teachers as you work over time to understand how technology use can improve instructional practice and increase student performance. Each chapter addresses a separate standard and its performance indicators, which are statements that more specifically describe the skill set for each standard. The material in this book is presented in a consistent format designed to assist you in understanding the performance indicators. Individual performance indicators are discussed in a narrative, followed by a table that prompts reflection on your instructional practice as related to the performance indicator. At the end of each chapter, you're asked to identify specific steps you can take immediately to increase or improve your practice as it relates to one performance indicator. It's assumed that over time, you'll revisit each standard and develop additional action steps related to the remaining performance indicators.

To reap the greatest benefit from this book, begin by reading the standards and their performance indicators carefully. This will give you an overview of the areas addressed by the standards. If you're looking for background information about a particular topic, the narrative for each performance indicator provides information and resources and will stand alone as a reference. If you're implementing a particular performance indicator, read the narrative and complete the table for that performance indicator as it pertains to your teaching assignment. Then use the Action Plan template at the end of the chapter to develop steps you'll take to implement that performance indicator. Those of you who are using the book with a partner or in a small group may decide to choose different performance indicators and then share your reflections and action steps.

If you're a preservice teacher candidate or a teacher with temporary credentials, you may first encounter this book during a formal course. Take advantage of this opportunity to discuss the narratives, reflective statements, and questions with your classmates. Then extend the discussion to experienced teachers you encounter in the course of your fieldwork or student teaching. Your action plan may be to incorporate what you learn here into assignments for methods courses and student teaching activities. Share your ideas and ask peers and instructors for feedback.

If you're a classroom teacher, you may receive this book during professional development training, as reading material for a professional learning community, or to read on your own. In a formalized setting, such as a training institute or professional learning community, a facilitator will probably guide you through readings and activities. Whether or not collaborative work is required, I encourage you to find at least one or two colleagues to work with. Discuss the narratives, reflective statements, and questions in your group, then work together to develop and implement the steps you will take to improve or expand your professional practice.

You can also use this book individually to increase personal knowledge and develop your own plan. However, if you're working alone you'll quickly find that you need support from co-workers to successfully implement a plan. In this case, the action plan may need to include strategies for garnering the support needed to make the plan work.

Most important, use this book to develop a coherent personal vision and action plans for technology use in your classroom.

NETS for Teachers

Educational Technology Standards and Performance Indicators for All Teachers

I. Technology Operations and Concepts

Teachers demonstrate a sound understanding of technology operations and concepts. Teachers:

- **A.** demonstrate introductory knowledge, skills, and understanding of concepts related to technology (as described in the ISTE National Educational Technology Standards for Students).
- **B.** demonstrate continual growth in technology knowledge and skills to stay abreast of current and emerging technologies.

II. Planning and Designing Learning Environments and Experiences

Teachers plan and design effective learning environments and experiences supported by technology. Teachers:

- **A.** design developmentally appropriate learning opportunities that apply technology-enhanced instructional strategies to support the diverse needs of learners.
- **B.** apply current research on teaching and learning with technology when planning learning environments and experiences.
- **C.** identify and locate technology resources and evaluate them for accuracy and suitability.
- **D.** plan for the management of technology resources within the context of learning activities.
- **E.** plan strategies to manage student learning in a technology-enhanced environment.

III. Teaching, Learning, and the Curriculum

Teachers implement curriculum plans that include methods and strategies for applying technology to maximize student learning. Teachers:

- **A.** facilitate technology-enhanced experiences that address content standards and student technology standards.
- **B.** use technology to support learner-centered strategies that address the diverse needs of students.
- **C.** apply technology to develop students' higher order skills and creativity.
- **D.** manage student learning activities in a technology-enhanced environment.

IV. Assessment and Evaluation

Teachers apply technology to facilitate a variety of effective assessment and evaluation strategies. Teachers:

- **A.** apply technology in assessing student learning of subject matter using a variety of assessment techniques.
- **B.** use technology resources to collect and analyze data, interpret results, and communicate findings to improve instructional practice and maximize student learning.
- **C.** apply multiple methods of evaluation to determine students' appropriate use of technology resources for learning, communication, and productivity.

V. Productivity and Professional Practice

Teachers use technology to enhance their productivity and professional practice. Teachers:

- **A.** use technology resources to engage in ongoing professional development and lifelong learning.
- **B.** continually evaluate and reflect on professional practice to make informed decisions regarding the use of technology in support of student learning.
- **C.** apply technology to increase productivity.
- **D.** use technology to communicate and collaborate with peers, parents, and the larger community in order to nurture student learning.

VI. Social, Ethical, Legal, and Human Issues

Teachers understand the social, ethical, legal, and human issues surrounding the use of technology in PK–12 schools and apply that understanding in practice. Teachers:

- **A.** model and teach legal and ethical practice related to technology use.
- **B.** apply technology resources to enable and empower learners with diverse backgrounds, characteristics, and abilities.
- **C.** identify and use technology resources that affirm diversity.
- **D.** promote safe and healthy use of technology resources.
- **E.** facilitate equitable access to technology resources for all students.

Chapter 1

STANDARD I

Technology Operations and Concepts

Teachers demonstrate a sound understanding of technology operations and concepts.

PERFORMANCE INDICATORS FOR TEACHERS

I.A. Demonstrate introductory knowledge, skills, and understanding of concepts related to technology (as described in the ISTE National Educational Technology Standards for Students).

I.B. Demonstrate continual growth in technology knowledge and skills to stay abreast of current and emerging technologies.

Chapter 1 Overview

The first standard in the National Educational Technology Standards for Teachers (NETS•T) overtly references the National Educational Technology Standards for Students (NETS•S), which were released by ISTE in June 1998. The NETS•S cover six broad areas:

1. Basic operations and concepts
2. Social, ethical, and human issues
3. Technology productivity tools
4. Technology communications tools
5. Technology research tools
6. Technology problem-solving and decision-making tools

Because Performance Indicator I.A. is based on the NETS•S, a brief overview of the student standards is provided below.

The NETS•S are intended to be used with students in Grades PK–12. This covers a lot of territory, so the standards are further defined through profiles that address grade-level clusters (PK–2, 3–5, 6–8, and 9–12). Each profile (available online at http://cnets.iste.org/students/s_profiles.html) includes age-appropriate performance indicators and curriculum-based scenarios. To see the big picture, you need to be familiar with all four profiles and become experts on the performance indicators for the specific grade-level cluster covering the grade(s) you teach. In addition, many districts also have their own student technology competencies that identify specific grade-level expectations for technology-literate students. You need to study these competencies to ensure that the necessary skills are being taught, measured, and documented.

But meeting the performance indicators for this standard requires more than simple awareness of the NETS•S. In addition to understanding the skills that comprise technology literacy for students, you must become technology literate yourself. The National Council for Accreditation of Teacher Education (NCATE) is the organization responsible for accrediting teacher credential programs in the United States. ISTE works closely with NCATE to make recommendations related to instructional technology and its role in teacher preparation to ensure that today's teacher candidates engage in coursework and activities designed to enable the incorporation of technology as a tool for teaching and learning.

In addition, ISTE and NCATE offer endorsements for exemplary programs that offer training in technology use beyond what's covered in basic credentialing courses. The Technology Facilitation (TF) Endorsement is awarded to programs that meet ISTE standards in preparing teacher candidates to serve as campus or building technology facilitators. If candidates enroll in TF-endorsed programs, they'll learn the skills needed to teach technology applications and demonstrate effective use of technology to support student learning of content. They'll also receive training in how to provide professional development, mentoring, and basic technical assistance to their colleagues.

A second ISTE/NCATE endorsement is for Technology Leadership (TL). Programs receiving this endorsement meet ISTE standards in preparing teacher candidates to act as technology coordinators, directors, or specialists at the district, regional, and state levels. In both cases, these programs allow candidates to earn an add-on endorsement to existing teaching credentials.

However, if you earned your credentials before these new requirements were in place, you still have a professional responsibility to meet the performance indicators for Standard I. In states where ongoing professional growth hours are required to renew teaching credentials, technology skills can (and should) be incorporated into every teacher's overall plan. If you hold life credentials and aren't required to earn ongoing credits to remain in the classroom, you still need to recognize that technology literacy is a fundamental responsibility of your job, not just another hurdle to jump over. Without these skills, it's no longer possible to provide relevant educational experiences to today's students.

Performance Indicator I.A. identifies the basic technology skills every classroom teacher needs to master. Performance Indicator I.B. reminds you that you need to engage in continual professional growth to keep these skills current.

Developing Basic Technology Literacy

Performance Indicator I.A.

Demonstrate introductory knowledge, skills, and understanding of concepts related to technology (as described in the ISTE National Educational Technology Standards for Students).

The National Educational Technology Standards Project offers a series of profiles for technology-literate teachers (available online at http://cnets.iste.org/teachers/t_profiles.html). Although written with preservice and first-year teachers in mind, the profile titled General Preparation is an excellent resource for inservice teachers who need to identify the technology literacy skills related to this performance indicator. The following is a list of the profile descriptors that relate to Performance Indicator I.A. and were adapted from the NETS•S:

1. Demonstrate a sound understanding of the nature and operation of technology systems.
2. Demonstrate proficiency in the use of common input and output devices; solve routine hardware and software problems; and make informed choices about technology systems, resources, and services.
3. Use content-specific tools (e.g., software, simulation, environmental probes, graphing calculators, exploratory environments, Web tools) to support learning and research.

4. Use technology resources to facilitate higher order and complex thinking skills, including problem solving, critical thinking, informed decision making, knowledge construction, and creativity.
5. Collaborate in constructing technology-enhanced models, preparing publications, and producing other creative works using productivity tools.
6. Use technology to locate, evaluate, and collect information from a variety of sources.
7. Use technology tools to process data and report results.
8. Use technology in the development of strategies for solving problems in the real world.
9. Evaluate and select new information resources and technological innovations based on their appropriateness to specific tasks.
10. Use a variety of media and formats, including telecommunications, to collaborate, publish, and interact with peers, experts, and other audiences.

Mastering these skills is the first step toward learning how to make effective use of technology a tool for teaching and learning.

You can begin by getting a clear picture of your level of skill in each of the areas listed above. Some states, such as California and Washington, now offer self-assessment tools teachers can use to develop a profile of technology skills. If you've completed a self-assessment within the last year, you can start by reviewing the results to identify areas of strength and need. Those of you who have never completed a self-assessment, or have not completed one within the last year, need to find out if your district has a tool in place. If one is available, it should be completed. If not, a variety of technology skills self-assessments designed specifically for teachers are available on the Web. For example, NetDay Compass offers an extensive list online at www.netdaycompass.org/categories.cfm?instance_id=54&category_id=4/.

Once a self-assessment has been completed, review the results with a critical eye and with grade-level or department team members. Use the profile to identify classes, seminars, workshops, and other professional development activities that would meet areas of need for individuals and the team. The discussion of Performance Indicator V.A. in chapter 5 includes several resources for effective professional development in technology literacy and strategies for working collaboratively that can also be used to strengthen the skills addressed here.

Use the statements in the following table to consider steps you might take to demonstrate introductory knowledge, skills, and understanding of concepts related to technology (as described in the ISTE National Educational Technology Standards for Students).

TABLE 1.1 ▪ Performance Indicator I.A.

Demonstrate introductory knowledge, skills, and understanding of concepts related to technology (as described in the ISTE National Educational Technology Standards for Students).

Directions: Give a Yes or No answer to statements 1–3. Based on your answers, respond to the appropriate additional items.

Statement	Yes	No
1. My district has a self-assessment tool that teachers use to rate their introductory knowledge, skills, and understanding of concepts related to technology.		
2. Teachers are expected to complete a self-assessment at least annually.		
3. I use the results of a self-assessment when developing my professional growth plan.		

If you answered Yes to at least one of the first three statements, respond to items 4 and 5.
4. Describe how the self-assessment results are used for professional growth:
5. Describe how use of the self-assessment results could be improved:

If you answered No to the first three statements, respond to items 6 and 7.
6. Review the self-assessment tools found on the NetDay Compass Web site (see resources section at end of chapter) and select a tool for your own use. Identify the tool you selected here:
7. Explain how you will use these results to increase your technology literacy skills:

Maintaining Technology Literacy through Ongoing Professional Development

Performance Indicator I.B.

Demonstrate continual growth in technology knowledge and skills to stay abreast of current and emerging technologies.

Effective technology integrators never stop learning about new, promising technologies. However, rapid changes in current and emerging technologies keep even the most enthusiastic users on their toes. Many districts and regional offices of education offer free or low-cost professional development designed to assist your continual growth in technology knowledge and skills. Convenience and customization to local needs are just two reasons it's worth checking to see what local training is available. An added bonus is the fact that those of you who attend these events may be able to earn continuing education credits.

Participation in classes, seminars, and workshops is one way to stay abreast of current and emerging technologies; however, you can use additional, less labor-intensive strategies to keep up-to-date in this rapidly changing field. For example, you can learn a great deal by

- becoming a member of a professional organization,
- reading print and online professional journals,
- subscribing to online news resources,
- participating in an online community, and
- posting to and reading education technology blogs.

One professional organization to consider joining is ISTE. Its mission is to advance the effective use of technology in education by providing leadership and services to its members. This organization offers an annual international conference, professional development opportunities, and an extensive list of publications that includes both books and journals. Members may join Special Interest Groups (SIGs) that target specific areas of interest. In addition, there's a national network of affiliate organizations, many of which offer regional conferences and other member benefits. Joining this kind of group provides you with up-to-date information and an international professional network.

Professional magazines and journals are also good resources for technology news. ISTE publishes *Journal of Research on Technology in Education* and *Learning & Leading with Technology*. Other well-known publications include *Technology & Learning*, *T.H.E. Journal*, and *Edutopia*. Each of these magazines also offers at least some, if not all, of its print content in an online format. See the resources section at the end of this chapter for links to these publications.

Want to stay on top of things, but don't have a lot of time? Identify a few online resources to skim regularly for updates on emerging technologies. Two very helpful online news briefs are eSchool News' eSN This Week (www.eschoolnews.com) and SmartBrief (www.smartbrief.com/ascd/), published by the Association for Supervision and Curriculum Development (ASCD). These free publications are e-mailed to readers in a digest format on a weekly or daily basis. Read the headlines and descriptors to get a general idea of the topic and click on the links provided to read more in-depth information.

You can also subscribe to a free aggregator such as Bloglines (www.bloglines.com). Aggregators allow subscribers to search for sites of interest and add them to a list. Then, when a selected site is updated, the aggregator notifies the subscriber. This makes it easy to track several news sources without having to check individual sites on a regular basis. In addition to education-related materials, you can learn a lot about trends in technology by reading the business section of any newspaper, or technology-related magazines such as *Wired* (http://wired.com). Again, much of this information is available online and can be subscribed to using an aggregator.

Use the questions in the following table to consider steps you might take to demonstrate continual growth in technology knowledge and skills to stay abreast of current and emerging technologies.

TABLE 1.2 ■ **Performance Indicator I.B.**

Demonstrate continual growth in technology knowledge and skills to stay abreast of current and emerging technologies.

Directions: Give a Yes or No answer to the following questions. Use the short-answer areas to respond to prompts or questions.

1. Are you a member of any professional organizations?	Yes	No
If you answered Yes to question 1, list those organizations here:		
In your opinion, what are the benefits and drawbacks of membership in a professional organization?		
2. Do you regularly read professional magazines or journals?	**Yes**	**No**
If you answered Yes to question 2, list those publications here:		

(Continued)

TABLE 1.2 ■ **Performance Indicator I.B.** *(Continued)*

	Yes	No
In your opinion, what are the benefits and drawbacks of regularly reading professional publications?		
3. Do you regularly read online information related to education technology (e.g., e-newsletters, blogs, etc.)?		
If you answered Yes to question 3, list those online information sources here:		
In your opinion, what are the benefits and drawbacks of regularly reading online information related to education technology?		
List 2–3 steps you will take to sustain continued growth in technology knowledge and skills to stay abreast of current and emerging technologies:		

Action Plan

Now that you've read about each performance indicator for Standard I and have had the opportunity to think about your level of implementation for each indicator, it's time to develop an action plan to improve or expand your professional practice in each area.

First, review your responses to the statements and questions in each performance indicator table. It's not possible to master every performance indicator at once, so choose one at a time. Build your plan by using the steps that you identified you might take for the chosen performance indicator and complete your action plan by using the table below. Performance Indicator I.B. has been used as a sample.

TABLE 1.3 ■ **Teachers demonstrate a sound understanding of technology operations and concepts**

Performance Indicator	Next Steps	I need to work on this step with the following people...	I will know this step has been achieved when...	Timeline
I.B. Demonstrate continual growth in technology knowledge and skills to stay abreast of current and emerging technologies.	*Find out about district policy on membership fees and join ISTE. Encourage other members of grade-level team to join as well.*	*Check with principal about policy and talk with grade-level team.*	*I have received membership materials and have visited ISTE's Web site.*	*1 month*
	1.			
	2.			
	3.			

Resources

PROFESSIONAL READING

Edutopia. Available: www.edutopia.org/magazine/

eSchool News. Available: www.eschoolnews.com

Journal of Research on Technology in Education. Available: www.iste.org/Content/NavigationMenu/Publications/JRTE/Issues/Volume_38/Number_3_Spring_2006/Number_3_Spring_2006.htm

Learning and Leading with Technology. Available: www.iste.org/Content/NavigationMenu/Publications/LL/LLIssues/Volume_33_2006_2005_/March_No_6_/March_2006.htm

SmartBrief. Available: www.smartbrief.com/ascd/

Technology & Learning. Available: www.techlearning.com

T.H.E. Journal. Available: http://thejournal.com

WEB SITES

Bloglines. Available: www.bloglines.com

International Society for Technology in Education. *Profiles for technology-literate students*. Available: http://cnets.iste.org/students/s_profiles.html

International Society for Technology in Education. *Profiles for technology-literate teachers*. Available: http://cnets.iste.org/teachers/t_profiles.html

NetDay Compass. *Resources*. Available: www.netdaycompass.org/categories.cfm?instance_id=54&category_id=4

Chapter 2

STANDARD II

Planning and Designing Learning Environments and Experiences

Teachers plan and design effective learning environments and experiences supported by technology.

PERFORMANCE INDICATORS FOR TEACHERS

II.A. Design developmentally appropriate learning opportunities that apply technology-enhanced instructional strategies to support the diverse needs of learners.

II.B. Apply current research on teaching and learning with technology when planning learning environments and experiences.

II.C. Identify and locate technology resources and evaluate them for accuracy and suitability.

II.D. Plan for the management of technology resources within the context of learning activities.

II.E. Plan strategies to manage student learning in a technology-enhanced environment.

Chapter 2 Overview

I've always been a proponent of appropriate use of technology as a tool for teaching and learning as opposed to using technology for its own sake. I still hold this belief; however, we've reached a point where educators' views of "best use" of technology and students' perceptions of "best use" are diverging significantly. The PowerPoint presentation posted on the National Education Technology Plan Web site includes the following quote from former U.S. Secretary of Education Rod Paige: "Education is the only business still debating the usefulness of technology."

Today's teachers must come to grips with the fact that accomplishing tasks using more traditional methods may still work, but this often leaves students cold. Why? Because outside the classroom students have access to technologies that allow them to do the same work in ways that make more sense to them. Instead of clinging to the way you learned to do things as students, you need to embrace real-world uses of technology and at least mirror, if not lead, that use in the classroom.

Standards II through IV address how teachers plan (Standard II), implement (Standard III), and assess (Standard IV) technology-supported instruction. There's a strong correlation among the performance indicators for these three standards. Read chapters 2, 3, and 4 carefully to identify the connections.

Designing Technology-Enhanced Learning Environments and Experiences

Performance Indicator II.A.

Design developmentally appropriate learning opportunities that apply technology-enhanced instructional strategies to support the diverse needs of learners.

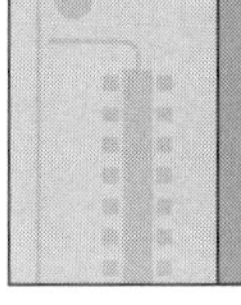

Performance Indicator II.B.

Apply current research on teaching and learning with technology when planning learning environments and experiences.

All five performance indicators for this standard are interdependent, but Performance Indicators II.A. and II.B. are particularly intertwined. Therefore, these two performance indicators are discussed together here.

To design learning opportunities that employ effective technology-enhanced instructional strategies, you must know what current research says about teaching and learning with technology. In addition, you must clearly understand how your personal views and use of technology influence your ability to use technology as a tool for teaching and learning. This is underscored in a report published by the SouthEast Initiatives Regional Technology in Education Consortium (2001) titled *Lessons Learned: Factors Influencing the Effective Use of Technology for Teaching and Learning.*

One finding in the report states, "Effective use of technology requires changes in teaching; in turn, the adoption of a new teaching strategy can be a catalyst for technology integration." In other words, teachers who are effective users of classroom technology have changed their approach to instruction and shifted to using technology as a learning tool.

This critical distinction is also found in the Apple Classrooms of Tomorrow Project (1995) research. This project ran from 1985 to 1995 and examined how teachers and students in target classrooms used technology over a period of time. One of the most important findings was that project teachers learned how to use technology in stages, and effective incorporation of technology as a tool for learning didn't enter into the picture until the later stages. The stages identified in this research are shown in table 2.1.

TABLE 2.1 ■ **Stages of educator learning**

STAGE	BEHAVIORS
Entry	Teacher is learning the basics of a technology, e.g., how to set up equipment and operate it.
Adoption	Teacher begins to use the technology in management areas, e.g., computer-generated quizzes or worksheets, grade books.
Adaptation	Teacher begins to use software to support instruction, e.g., a commercially produced content area program or productivity tools (word processor, database).
Appropriation	Teacher begins to focus on collaborative, project-based technology use, and technology becomes one of several instructional tools.
Invention	Teacher begins to develop different uses for technology, e.g., creates projects that combine two or more technologies.

Source: Data adapted from Apple Classrooms of Tomorrow Project (1995).

Another significant factor is the growing recognition that the majority of adults over the age of 30 (teachers included) view most aspects of technology use quite differently than do people younger than 30. This is because they didn't grow up as technology users. Prensky (2001, October) coined the term *digital immigrant* to describe people who first learned how to use technology as adults. He explains that learning to use technology in adulthood is similar to learning how to speak a new language at the same age. It's still possible to become proficient in the language, but most adult learners will have at least a slight accent.

By the same token, digital immigrants can learn to use new technologies, but they often unconsciously limit this learning to automation of familiar tasks, ignoring other capabilities that would ultimately enable them to approach tasks in new or different ways. Prensky calls this a *digital accent.* Teachers who doubt the existence of digital accents need only think about the number of adults who print online articles before reading them.

Although it's not necessarily their intent, digital immigrants often limit students' use of technology even when access isn't an issue. Students may be required to write a rough draft by hand before being allowed to use a word processor. Or students may be provided laptops to take notes and then told to keep the lid closed during direct instruction so that the teacher can be sure they're paying attention. These are just two of many ways digital accents can impede classroom technology use. However, you can make effective use of technology as a tool for learning when you recognize your digital accents and adjust for them.

Research on Effective Use of Technology as a Tool for Teaching and Learning

It's often said there isn't much research showing that technology use has any impact on teaching or student learning. That may have been true a decade ago, but today, it's simply not the case. Numerous studies examine the use of technology as a teaching and learning tool. The resources section at the end of the chapter has links to some of this research. Here's a summary of the major findings:

1. Teachers make more effective use of technology as an instructional tool when
    - technology use is systemically included in lesson and unit plans, providing information about the hardware and applications used and how this supports instructional objectives and students' learning needs;
    - they make sure students have acquired basic proficiency with the technology prior to using it in a content-based lesson;
    - the technology is used to extend or reinforce core curricula; and
    - school site plans describe in detail how technology is used to support curriculum, instruction, and administration.
2. There's a positive impact on academic performance when
    - student use of technology is supported by teachers, administrators, and parents;
    - technology use is integrated throughout the school day;
    - the application used has a direct correlation to the curriculum objectives being assessed;
    - the application adjusts the level of difficulty and provides feedback based on individual students' needs;
    - students have opportunities to work collaboratively while using the technology; and
    - students have opportunities to design and implement content-related projects.

Couple these findings with the information about teacher use of technology provided earlier in this chapter, and we begin to understand the multiple ways educators can use technology as a teaching and learning tool.

Getting Started

The following table includes steps you might take to ensure you're planning for effective use of technology.

TABLE 2.2 ■ **Planning for effective use of technology**

STEP	EXAMPLE
1. Based on the site technology plan and curriculum objectives, consider whether technology use would be appropriate as a teaching tool.	Technology performance indicator from site plan: Use technology tools for individual and collaborative writing, communication, and publishing activities to create knowledge products for audiences inside and outside the classroom. English/language arts performance indicators: Create simple documents by using electronic media and employing organizational features (e.g., passwords, entry and pull-down menus, word searches, thesaurus, spelling checker). Edit and revise manuscripts to improve the meaning and focus of writing by adding, deleting, consolidating, clarifying, and rearranging words and sentences.
2. Choose a familiar technology or a feature of an application that can be used to meet the objectives.	Editing features of a word processor (e.g., Track Changes, Cut, Copy, Paste, Spelling and Grammar)
3. Design a teaching activity.	Model use of editing features (e.g., Track Changes, Cut, Copy, Paste, Spelling and Grammar) during daily language exercises. Use teacher presentation station and word processor to project sentences students need to correct. After students have corrected sentences independently, brainstorm corrections using the editing features. Discuss all suggestions and accept or reject edits using Track Changes. Compile exercises into a file that's printed and distributed to students each week.
4. How does this activity demonstrate effective use of technology as a teaching tool?	Daily use becomes systemic and provides opportunities to model technology skills while addressing specific content area skills. Weekly printouts ensure that students have a common language reference for writing essays.
5. Can these same technology skills be used as a learning tool to extend or reinforce the curriculum objectives?	Students write a brief essay each week that incorporates skills covered in daily language exercises. Students dislike editing the essays. Reserve the mobile laptop lab twice each week so students can word process their essays and work individually or in small groups to edit one another's writing using the editing features modeled during daily language exercises. This meets the standards listed above.
6. Review student learning profiles and technology skills.	A few students prefer to do this kind of activity independently. The remaining students work well in trios. The trios can be heterogeneous so that students with stronger skills can assist others. (Intelligences: Verbal, Interpersonal, Intrapersonal.) All students know how to create a word processing document, enter text, and use the Cut, Copy, and Paste commands. Students need direct instruction in how to use Track Changes and Spelling and Grammar.
7. How does this activity demonstrate effective use of technology as a learning tool?	Use will become systemic. Students have an opportunity to use technology in a way that is directly related to curriculum objectives. As they work collaboratively, groups will decide how they want to approach the task of editing the files.

Using these steps may seem artificial at first. However, with practice it becomes easier to think in these terms while planning. When this occurs, use of technology-based tools becomes one of many strategies you regularly consider when designing lessons and learning activities.

Many resources offer ideas for technology-supported, content-based activities. For example, ISTE publishes a variety of journals and books that address this topic. Browse these materials by going to www.iste.org and clicking on the Publications link. Other useful links are Internet4Classrooms' Integrated Technology Lesson Plans (www.Internet4classrooms.com/integ_tech_lessons.htm), AT&T Knowledge Network Explorer's Blue Web'N (www.filamentality.com/wired/blueWebn/), and TrackStar (http://trackstar.4teachers.org/trackstar/).

The following table provides steps you might take to increase your ability to design developmentally appropriate learning opportunities that apply technology-enhanced instructional strategies to support learners' diverse needs. The table also has steps for using current research on teaching and learning with technology when planning learning environments and experiences.

TABLE 2.3 ■ Performance Indicators II.A. and II.B.

II.A. Design developmentally appropriate learning opportunities that apply technology-enhanced instructional strategies to support the diverse needs of learners.

II.B. Apply current research on teaching and learning with technology when planning learning environments and experiences.

Directions: Rate each numbered statement using the scale provided. Use the short-answer areas to respond to prompts or questions.

Rating Scale: **1** = Never **2** = Seldom **3** = Sometimes **4** = Often **5** = Regularly (as appropriate)					
1. Current research on teaching and learning with technology is considered when planning learning environments and experiences.	1	2	3	4	5
Describe how current research on teaching and learning with technology is considered when planning learning environments and experiences:					
List two useful resources for current research on teaching and learning with technology:					
How could you increase or improve the use of research in planning? List at least two action steps you will take:					

(Continued)

TABLE 2.3 ■ **Performance Indicators II.A. and II.B.** *(Continued)*

2. Appropriate technology-supported teaching strategies are incorporated into lessons to enhance instruction.	1	2	3	4	5
Describe how appropriate technology-supported teaching strategies are incorporated into lessons to enhance instruction:					
List 2–3 steps you will take to increase or improve incorporation of appropriate technology-supported teaching strategies into lessons to enhance instruction:					

3. Developmentally appropriate technology-supported learning strategies are incorporated into lesson plans to support the diverse needs of learners.	1	2	3	4	5
Describe how developmentally appropriate technology-enhanced learning strategies are incorporated into lesson plans to support the diverse needs of learners:					
List 2–3 steps you will take to increase or improve the incorporation of developmentally appropriate technology-supported learning strategies into lesson plans to support the diverse needs of learners:					

Locating and Evaluating Technology Resources

Performance Indicator II.C.

Identify and locate technology resources and evaluate them for accuracy and suitability.

Reading product reviews, visiting vendors in the exhibit hall during conferences, and soliciting recommendations from colleagues are just a few ways to stay current on available technology resources. Online publications such as *techLEARNING* (http://techlearning.com), *Learning & Leading with Technology* (www.iste.org, click on Publications), *T.H.E. Journal* (www.thejournal.com), and *eSchool News* (http://eschoolnews.com) regularly offer product reviews and information in print and online. Web sites, including EvaluTech (www.evalutech.sreb.org) and the California Learning Resource Network (www.clrn.org), are also helpful. However, don't rely solely on the opinions of others.

The best way to evaluate a new technology is to try it out in the environment where it will be used. Many software publishers now offer demo programs that can be downloaded and reviewed for 30 days. Others allow potential customers to order a software package or piece of equipment on a 30-day trial basis. Ask the principal and tech support staff if it's permissible for teachers to use either of these options when reviewing new products. If not, find out what other options are available.

It's helpful to use a software review form when evaluating a new program because the items included provide a checklist that helps ensure a thorough review. Also, notes taken during the evaluation help jog the reviewer's memory when, after reviewing several items, it's time to make a choice. Completed reviews then become resources for subsequent use by other reviewers and help answer questions about why something was (or wasn't) selected.

Districts sometimes develop their own evaluation forms, but if you don't have access to a district form, you can easily find sample forms online. For example, the Educational Software Evaluation Form developed by ISTE is available at http://cnets.iste.org/teachers/pdf/App_D_Software.pdf.

Kathy Schrock's Software Evaluation Form at http://kathyschrock.net/1computer/page4.htm is also a good tool for this purpose.

Hardware review is another matter altogether. As district and site networks expand in size and complexity, security and compatibility issues increase as well. Districts often establish minimum specification standards, but so many variables must be taken into account that it's usually best to work with both instructional and tech support staff when evaluating new hardware. Why both? Because decisions about adoptions of new hardware must be based on what's instructionally sound and technically practical. Engaging representatives from both arenas at the outset can save time and help ensure sound decisions.

You also need to become skilled at locating and evaluating online resources. Online search engines are easier to use today than ever before, but there are tips and tricks that help target searches more effectively. To learn more about the capabilities of a particular search engine, go to its home page and look for a link called Help, Advanced Search Techniques, or something similar. For example, Google's home page has an Advanced Search link so that users can refine searches to include specific file formats, publication dates, or languages, and more. Scroll to the bottom of the home page and click on Help to find an index of short articles that answer frequently asked questions (FAQs).

Web-Based Bookmarking Services

Most computer users know how to use their Web browser's Favorites or Bookmarking command to save a Web site in the computer's desktop. While this is a handy feature, access to the list of sites saved is restricted to the individual computer. Free Web-based bookmarking services such as Backflip.com (www.backflip.com) enable you to access bookmarked sites from any Internet-connected computer. Several of these services, including del.icio.us (http://del.icio.us/) even allow you to share your bookmark lists with others. This means you can easily share sites with colleagues and students. A Google search using the keywords "Web-based bookmarking" yields a lengthy list of services to choose from. To get started, subscribe to an account and follow the directions provided by that service.

Online resources range from full courses, to individual Web sites with information that supports curricular concepts, to supplemental materials and e-books posted by textbook publishers. Some of these materials are free, while others are fee-based. Once resources are located, it's important to take the time to review them carefully. Virtually anyone who has the skills and access can post information online, regardless of their level of expertise or credentials, so it's best to have a critical eye. Unlike hard-copy publications, where even physical appearance can provide clues about the reliability of the information (think tabloid compared to a copy of the *New York Times*), Web site design is not necessarily indicative of content quality. There are many hoax Web sites on the Web today. Some are fairly obvious, such as Save the Pacific Northwest Tree Octopus (http://zapatopi.net/treeoctopus/) or Fun Phone (www.funphone.com/old/). But others, such as Dihydrogen Monoxide Research Division (www.dhmo.org) and Fakes and Originals (www.saskschools.ca/~ischool/tisdale/integrated/wysiwyg/assignment_1.htm), take more time to identify.

You should consider several elements when evaluating online resources. Table 2.4 provides a list of evaluation criteria.

The Web offers many sample online-resource review tools. For example, Kathy Schrock's Guide for Educators includes the Critical Evaluation Information page at http://school.discovery.com/schrockguide/eval.html. It features rubrics and articles related to Web site evaluation.

TABLE 2.4 ■ **Suggested Web site evaluation criteria**

	QUESTIONS TO ASK	WHAT TO LOOK FOR
Source	Was the material prepared by a reliable person or organization? How do you know? Is contact information provided?	The URL will reveal if this is a personal site or one hosted by an education, government, nonprofit, or commercial entity. The name of the author or organization should appear on the home page. An About Us link should provide additional background information. A Contact Us link should provide at least an e-mail address and telephone number.
Material	Is the information that's presented original, or is it a collection of links? Is the information current? Are resources clearly cited? How accurate is the material?	Look for reliable outside links. Multiple broken or weak links detract from the reliability of the original site. Each page (usually at the bottom) should have a Last Updated notation. Look for footnotes, bibliographies, or links that provide supporting documentation. Examine additional online and offline sources to verify material.
Site design	Is the site easy to navigate? Can useful information be retrieved quickly? Do visuals enhance or detract?	Links to other pages in the site should be easy to see and clearly identified. As a rule, you should be able get what you need in 3–4 clicks. Pages should be visually attractive but not cluttered. The number of graphics should not noticeably impact the time it takes for pages to load for viewing.
Access	Is the site free or fee-based? Have accommodations been made for users with physical or learning disabilities?	Double-check that subscription information is linked to the home page; it generally is. Examine the Terms of Use to determine if you want to sign up for an account. Look for a notice stating Bobby or WebXACT approval (indicates the site has been checked for accessibility). Watch for items that may impact users with disabilities, including font size, color scheme, page layout, auditory content, etc.
Advertising	Is the site ad-free?	Take notice of advertising. Students are easily influenced by ads, and some districts prohibit use of Web sites that include ads. If sites with ads are permissible, make sure the ad content is appropriate for students.

It's important to remember that many online teaching resources, particularly lesson plans, have little or nothing to do with effective use of technology. This means that if you're looking specifically for lessons that model effective technology use, you may need to sift through a number of lesson plans before finding good materials. Plan ahead and develop a plan for book-marking promising lessons for later retrieval. Lesson plan sites referenced earlier in the chapter are also appropriate resources to explore when implementing this performance indicator.

Use the questions in table 2.5 to consider steps that might be taken to increase your ability to identify and locate technology resources and evaluate them for accuracy and suitability.

TABLE 2.5 ■ **Performance Indicator II.C.**
Identify and locate technology resources and evaluate them for accuracy and suitability.

Directions: Give a Yes or No answer to questions 1 and 2. Use the short-answer areas to elaborate on your answers.

1. Does the district have policies for software, hardware, and online resource reviews?	Yes	No
If your answer is Yes, describe your district's policies for software, hardware, and online resource reviews:		
Do these policies help or hinder teachers? Explain:		
2. Does the district provide forms for evaluating software, hardware, and online resources?	**Yes**	**No**
If your answer is Yes, describe how these forms are used:		
What kind of support do teachers need to effectively evaluate new technology resources? Explain:		

Planning Lessons That Make Effective Use of Learning Technologies

Performance Indicator II.D.

Plan for the management of technology resources within the context of learning activities.

If you're not an experienced technology user, or aren't confident in your troubleshooting skills, you'll need to take more time initially to plan lessons that incorporate the use of technology resources. In addition to thinking about how the content will be addressed, you'll need to plan for the mechanics of dealing with equipment and software or other instructional materials. However, this need to take extra time will diminish as your level of technology proficiency grows.

If you use reflective journaling to document your implementation of new lessons, you'll find that it's easier to return to the lesson at a later date and remember what you did, what worked well, and what needed revision before presenting the lesson again. When planning how you'll manage technology resources within the context of learning activities, you'll need to consider several factors in several areas.

Hardware

Once you've identified a lesson where use of technology would enhance or enrich the content, it's time to ask several practical questions about the equipment needed:

1. What technology will be used?
2. Is the technology available on-site, or will it need to be borrowed or checked out from another location?
3. Is the technology available when needed?
4. Where will the technology be used?
5. How will this location limit or enable use of this technology?

These questions are important because they'll help you think through the basics and avoid making assumptions. Start with a list of what's needed. If the technology is available in the classroom, it should be easy to answer the remaining questions. However, if the equipment must be borrowed or used in a lab, don't assume that a piece of equipment will necessarily be available. Things break, disappear, or are scheduled for use elsewhere. Be sure to check on availability and scheduling requirements well ahead of time.

Think through how you plan to use the technology and how your location might impact this use. For example, bringing a mobile lab of laptops or handheld computers into the classroom provides more flexibility in where and how the equipment is used, but this may also mean that you'll have to ensure that batteries have been charged before the lesson. If you want to use the Internet, it might be necessary to use a lab, depending on what kind of online access is available and the quality of the connection. Time may also be a factor, particularly if students must leave the classroom and boot up equipment before they can actually get started on the lesson. This is an especially important consideration for teachers on a 50- or 60-minute class schedule.

Another issue may be the arrangement of the physical space where students will be working. Is the layout conducive to a variety of instructional groupings, or are options limited? Is the teaching station in a convenient location where it's easy to observe students at work, or is it difficult to move around the room to monitor progress? None of these issues are insurmountable, but they do need to be considered before teaching the lesson.

If the space isn't ideal due to furniture arrangement, you can temporarily move desks, tables, and chairs to achieve desired learning groupings and flow of traffic. Structural issues such as lines of sight obstructed by support pillars (often found in large labs or media centers) are more difficult to control, but preplanning still helps. If possible, either steer students away from workstations with poor sightlines or structure activities so that students don't need to constantly direct their attention toward the front of the room.

Instructional Materials (Software and Online Resources)

In addition to thinking about hardware, it's important to take the time to make plans about the software and online resources required. Here are several questions to consider:

1. What technology-based instructional materials will be used?
2. Are the materials to be used compatible with the available hardware?
3. If software is included in the plan, is it installed on every computing device?
4. If online resources are included in the plan, how will students be accessing this information (e.g., using bookmarks, hotlists, search engines, etc.)?
5. If online resources are included in the plan, have URLs been checked for accuracy and availability?

Again, don't make assumptions. Once you've selected the materials, make sure they're available and working. Newer software doesn't always run on older computers. Schools sometimes have multiple versions of software programs, which may lead to confusion in the classroom, especially if one student's screen looks different from a neighbor's but both are engaged in the same activity.

Also, schools don't always purchase enough licenses to have every program installed on every machine. Teachers need to check licensing restrictions before installing programs on new or additional machines. You may also need to work with technical support staff to acquire software installation rights on the network if they're not available to do the install themselves.

When using online resources, make certain they're accessible at school. That wonderful site you found on your home computer may be blocked by the district filter, or the online lesson that worked well last year may flop today because the link is no longer available. Bookmark specific sites or create a hotlist so that students aren't wasting time typing and retyping Internet addresses to access sites. Online tools such as Filamentality and TrackStar (see the resources section at the end of the chapter) are easy to use, and they enable teachers to create Web-based activities with links built right in.

FIGURE 2.1 Using Web-based Filamentality templates, you can easily create a variety of online activities with embedded links for student use.

Troubleshooting

No matter how much preplanning is done, there's always the chance that something will go wrong. What happens when a piece of equipment doesn't work, when the network goes down, or when the software locks up? When using a new piece of equipment or a new program, it's worth taking time to meet with technical support staff to review how to use the technology and learn simple troubleshooting techniques. Many of these skills are transferable, so once you've learned how to handle a situation with one piece of equipment or program, the same troubleshooting skills will often work in other circumstances.

Think about how to handle the immediate situation first and then troubleshoot later to make sure the problem doesn't happen again. Learn your district's or site's procedures for getting assistance, and follow those procedures.

Always have a backup plan. Yes, the goal is to use technology to engage students and use information in new, inventive ways; and this should mean that your lessons become increasingly technology-immersed. However, remember when the film didn't get delivered or a torrential rain meant scrapping an outdoor activity? When these things happen, teachers don't decide to abandon showing films or confine all lessons to indoor environments. It's the same with technology use. As your level of confidence with technology grows, your ability to make adjustments in technology use will also increase. Students understand and respect a teacher's willingness to try, even when something goes wrong.

Use the following table to consider steps that might be taken to increase your ability to plan for the management of technology resources within the context of learning activities.

TABLE 2.6 ■ Performance Indicator II.D.

Plan for the management of technology resources within the context of learning activities.

Directions: Rate each numbered statement using the scale provided. Use the short-answer areas to respond to prompts or questions.

Rating Scale: **1** = Never **2** = Seldom **3** = Sometimes **4** = Often **5** = Regularly (as appropriate)					
1. I specifically plan for the management of hardware use within the context of learning activities.	1	2	3	4	5
Management strategies for hardware use within the context of learning activities include:					
List 2–3 steps you'll take to increase or improve planning for the management of hardware use within the context of learning activities:					
2. I specifically plan for the management of technology-based instructional materials within the context of learning activities.	1	2	3	4	5
Management strategies employed for the use of technology-based instructional materials within the context of learning activities include:					

(Continued)

TABLE 2.6 ■ **Performance Indicator II.D.** *(Continued)*

List 2–3 steps you'll take to increase or improve planning for the management of technology-based instructional materials within the context of learning activities:					
3. I specifically plan for ways to troubleshoot problems when using technology resources within the context of learning activities.	1	2	3	4	5
Troubleshooting strategies employed include:					
List 2–3 steps you'll take to increase or improve planning strategies to troubleshoot problems when using technology resources within the context of learning activities:					

Improving Student Learning with Technology

Performance Indicator II.E.

Plan strategies to manage student learning in a technology-enhanced environment.

This is where many teachers become stymied. Refer back to the Apple Classrooms of Tomorrow (ACOT) study mentioned earlier in this chapter in the discussion of Performance Indicators II.A. and II.B. Typically, when teachers begin to use technology as a tool for instruction, they first use the technology for task management and then explore ways to automate traditional lessons. The same thing happens when teachers begin using technology as a learning tool for students. The natural inclination is to automate lesson activities. Students aren't asked to approach subject matter in a different way; rather, they're asked to use technology to do the same things, just a little faster.

For example, students will be asked to use a word processor to type a final copy of an essay instead of copying it by hand. Or, they're told to use a five-slide PowerPoint template instead of making a display board for a science fair project. Drill and practice software is used in lieu of flashcards and worksheets to review discrete skills in reading or math. While these automated activities may engage some students (at least initially), we cannot attribute any changes in overall student performance to this kind of technology use because the learning process itself hasn't changed.

The ACOT findings show that technology use does have an impact on student learning when it reaches the appropriation and invention stages. This doesn't mean you should avoid all adoption- and adaptation-stage activities, but it does mean you need to understand clearly what you're trying to accomplish instructionally, as well as how technology use at that level supports those goals.

Districts that accept Title II, Part D, of No Child Behind are required to measure students' levels of technology proficiency in eighth grade. These districts must also document how technology use is incorporated throughout the curriculum. The impact of these requirements filters down to the classroom. You may be asked to maintain profiles of students' skill levels in using technology and document use of research-based, technology-supported instruction. These requirements align well with the stages of use identified in ACOT, as well as with the spirit of this performance indicator.

Student Technology Skills

While students may in general be more adept than their teachers at using various technologies, they're often self-taught and have gaps in what they can and cannot do. It's important to assess your students' general technology skills to know where direct instruction in hardware, software, or technology-based instructional materials will be necessary before students will be able to use the technology as a tool for learning. In these cases, lessons need to include activities at the adoption stage to get students up to speed on the technology. Is this a waste of time? Not at all; many districts have created or adopted a scope and sequence of technology skills for students. Here are links to two examples:

- Kent School District's Technology Learning Outcomes—
www.kent.k12.wa.us/curriculum/tech/student_standards/k12chart.html
- Learning Point Associates' Student Technology Literacy Proficiency Checklist—
www.aea8.k12.ia.us/documents/u_031404213821.pdf

These skills must be taught at some point, and it makes sense to teach them when meaningful content-based lessons immediately follow the skill instruction. Once students have acquired new technical skills, they'll be able to use these skills again and again. The first step in managing student learning in a technology-enhanced environment, then, is making sure students have mastered the basic skills.

Troubleshooting Routines

Even after direct skills instruction, some students will need additional assistance using the technology. How can this be accommodated?

Just as routines are established for answering questions and providing assistance in other classroom activities, they must also be established for technology-supported lessons. Establish a sequence of steps for students to take when they need help. The first step may be for students to try to solve the problem on their own, using teacher-created step sheets that include screenshots and simple written directions. Step sheets can be created for virtually any program or Web site. Several sample step sheets for Microsoft Office programs may be downloaded at www.portical.org/tools/msoffice2000_stepsheets.html. The second step may be to ask a neighbor for assistance, using the step sheet. The third step may be to ask a designated student expert among a handful of students who are proficient in the skills and willing to help their peers.

If these steps don't correct the problem, the final step may be to ask an adult for assistance. Post these steps in the classroom along with a list of basic troubleshooting tips, and then encourage students to develop self-sufficiency by using them.

Technology as a Learning Tool

Once students have learned the prerequisite technology skills, they can engage in activities using technology to enhance or expand their learning. Refer again to the ACOT stages of use in table 2.1. Begin by developing activities where students are working at the adaptation stage. This allows you to introduce and explore academic content, and it offers students additional practice in using the technology. You can introduce concepts using a teaching station, then ask students to engage in technology-supported guided activities.

At this point, all of your students will likely be engaged in the same or similar activities at the same time. How will this be managed? Will all students use the technology as part of a large group activity, or will students rotate through learning centers where technology use is just one of several activities over a period of time? Will students have opportunities to use the technology individually?

In addition to the troubleshooting routines established during adoption-stage activities, you should institute procedures for completing and turning in work on time. Because initial activities will most likely be automations of fairly traditional lessons, regular classroom procedures may apply. However, it's important to review those procedures with regard to how students will document completed work. Who will they go to with content-related questions? How will you monitor students as they work? What is the backup plan?

Today, most teachers limit student use of technology as a learning tool to the adaptation stage. Unfortunately, research has shown that use of technology at this level has little or no impact on student performance. To learn effectively with technology, students must have opportunities to work at the appropriation and invention stages, engaging in projects that demonstrate content knowledge and mastery of technology skills. To be successful at this, students and teachers must first have basic technology skills and some confidence in their ability to solve technological problems.

When working at the appropriation stage, technology becomes one of several learning tools students use collaboratively to complete a project. Students typically work in cooperative groups, and each group may be using a different technology to complete a task. To accomplish this, you must be confident that your students have the technological and academic skills to work independently.

At the invention stage, students begin to identify new or different ways to use one or more technologies to solve problems. You may pose a question or problem and ask students to decide how they'll approach the task at hand, leaving it up to them to choose from a variety of work groupings, technologies, and learning resources. At this point you truly become a facilitator, providing support rather than direct instruction.

Management routines require careful thought at these last two levels. How will groups be formed? What are each member's responsibilities? How will work be documented and evaluated? How will you monitor multiple groups working on different activities? Activities of this scope tend to be long-term projects, extending over a quarter, a semester, perhaps even the entire year.

Use the questions in the following table to consider steps that might be taken to increase your ability to plan strategies to manage student learning in a technology-enhanced environment.

TABLE 2.7 ■ **Performance Indicator II.E.**

Plan strategies to manage student learning in a technology-enhanced environment.

Directions: Give Yes or No answers to questions 1 and 2, and use the short-answer areas to respond to prompts for question 2. Use the short-answer areas to respond to prompts 3–6.

	Yes	No
1. Has the district adopted a scope and sequence of technology skills for students?		
2. Are teachers required to maintain profiles for individual students' levels of technology skills?		
If profiles exist, explain how they are used to inform instruction:		
If profiles do not exist, explain how teachers assess student technology skills and use this information to inform instruction:		
3. List the three most commonly used technology-supported learning activities used in your classroom. Identify the ACOT stage for each activity listed:		
4. Describe troubleshooting strategies you and your students use when engaged in technology-supported learning activities:		
5. Describe your classroom management plan for handling technology-supported learning activities:		
6. List 2–3 action steps that you will take to increase or enhance your ability to manage student learning in a technology-enhanced environment:		

Action Plan

Now that you've read about each performance indicator for Standard II and have had the opportunity to think about your level of implementation for each indicator, it's time to develop an action plan to improve or expand your professional practice in this area.

First, review your responses to the statements and questions in each performance indicator table. It's not possible to master every performance indicator at once, so choose one at a time. Build your plan by using the steps you identified you might take for the chosen performance indicator and complete your action plan by using the table below. Performance Indicator II.A. has been used as a sample.

TABLE 2.8 ■ **Teachers plan and design effective learning environments and experiences supported by technology**

Performance Indicator	Next Steps	I need to work on this step with the following people...	I will know this step has been achieved when...	Timeline
II.A. Design developmentally appropriate learning opportunities that apply technology-enhanced instructional strategies to support the diverse needs of learners.	*Use table 2.2 in this chapter to modify an existing instructional unit to include adaptation-stage technology use.*	*District technology instructional specialist, site library/media specialist, other teachers at my grade level.*	*The modified instructional unit is ready for use with students.*	*2 weeks*
	1.			
	2.			
	3.			

Resources

ARTICLES AND REPORTS

Apple Classrooms of Tomorrow Project. (1995). *ACOT's 10 Year Report.* [Online report]. Available: www.apple.com/education/k12/leadership/acot/library.html

National Education Technology Plan. (2005). [Online report]. Available: www.ed.gov/about/offices/list/os/technology/plan/2004/site/edlite-default.html

Prensky, Marc. (2001, October). *Digital natives, digital immigrants.* [Online article]. Available: www.marcprensky.com/writing/Prensky%20-%20Digital%20Natives,%20Digital%20Immigrants%20-%20Part1.pdf

SouthEast Initiatives Regional Technology in Education Consortium. (2001). *Lessons learned: Factors influencing the effective use of technology for teaching and learning.* [Online report]. Available: www.seirtec.org/publications/lessons.pdf

ONLINE PUBLICATIONS

eSchool News. Available: http://eschoolnews.com

Learning & Leading with Technology. Available: www.iste.org/LL/

T.H.E. Journal. Available: www.thejournal.com

techLEARNING. Available: http://techlearning.com

PRODUCT REVIEWS AND EVALUATION FORMS

California Learning Resource Network. Available: www.clrn.org

EvaluTech. Available: www.evalutech.sreb.org

International Society for Technology in Education, *Educational Software Evaluation Form.* Available: http://cnets.iste.org/teachers/pdf/App_D_Software.pdf

Schrock, K. *Critical Evaluation Information.* Available: http://school.discovery.com/schrockguide/eval.html

Schrock, K. *Software Evaluation Form.* Available: http://kathyschrock.net/1computer/page4.htm

RESEARCH SITES

International Society for Technology in Education (ISTE), *Center for Applied Research in Educational Technology.* Available: http://caret.iste.org

North Central Regional Educational Laboratory (NCREL). Available: www.ncrel.org

PBS TeacherSource, *Technology & Teaching.* Available: www.pbs.org/teachersource/teachtech/research.shtm

U.S. Department of Education, Office of Educational Technology, *Evaluation and Research.* Available: www.ed.gov/about/offices/list/os/technology/evaluation.html

ONLINE TOOLS AND LESSONS

AT& T Knowledge Network Explorer's Blue Web'N.
Available: www.filamentality.com/wired/blueWebn/

AT& T Knowledge Network Explorer's Filamentality.
Available: www.filamentality.com/wired/fil/

International Society for Technology in Education. Available: www.iste.org

Internet4Classrooms, Integrated Technology Lesson Plans.
Available: www.Internet4classrooms.com/integ_tech_lessons.htm

University of Kansas, TrackStar.
Available: http://trackstar.4teachers.org/trackstar/

SAMPLE STEP SHEETS

York, C., *Microsoft Office 2000 Step Sheets.*
Available: www.portical.org/tools/msoffice2000_stepsheets.html

Chapter 3

STANDARD III

Teaching, Learning, and the Curriculum

Teachers implement curriculum plans that include methods and strategies for applying technology to maximize student learning.

PERFORMANCE INDICATORS FOR TEACHERS

III.A. Facilitate technology-enhanced experiences that address content standards and student technology standards.

III.B. Use technology to support learner-centered strategies that address the diverse needs of students.

III.C. Apply technology to develop students' higher order skills and creativity.

III.D. Manage student learning activities in a technology-enhanced environment.

Chapter 3 Overview

Eighteenth-century poet Robert Burns wrote, "The best laid schemes o' mice an' men / Gang aft a-gley" (often go awry). So it can go with lesson plans. You often have the best intentions for implementing new or enhanced instructional methods and strategies and then, for a variety of reasons, end up falling back on familiar practices instead. This is particularly true when technology use is involved.

Problems with the infrastructure, the need to deal with new classroom management issues, and inconsistent technology skill levels among teachers and students are barriers that can lead to under-use of technology, despite what's written in the plan book. Careful planning helps, but it's difficult to anticipate how well a new lesson will work until it's actually implemented. Standard III reminds you that it's important to regularly use technology tools in teaching and learning.

I often hear educators say their time is limited and too many demands are already placed on them. It's absolutely true that your workload is far greater now than it was in the past. However, it's also true that your job is to prepare today's students for their future, not your past. To do this, you must use the kinds of tools and learning experiences that will help students develop marketable 21st-century skills. It's doubtful this can be accomplished in a technology-free environment.

Addressing Content Area and Technology Standards in the Classroom

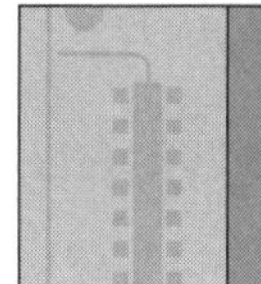

Performance Indicator III.A.

Facilitate technology-enhanced experiences that address content standards and student technology standards.

Facilitation of standards-based, technology-enhanced experiences requires the kind of in-depth planning and preparation described in chapter 2. You must have thorough knowledge of academic and technology standards, as well as a clear picture of how students will use their technology skills to support content learning.

This is an important distinction, because traditionally, student technology use hasn't necessarily been associated with achievement of curricular goals and objectives, except for the rudimentary skills needed to use drill-and-practice software or tutorials. Students march off to the computer lab or enroll in computer skills electives, where skills are taught in isolation. In cases where a special instructor teaches technology skills, regular classroom teachers may have little or no knowledge of what technology skills are being covered. Even in those instances where teachers communicate regularly with the computer lab instructor or provide the instruction in technology skills themselves, they may not be making the connection between those skills and their application in academic activities. As a result, student technology skills are often viewed as an add-on rather than as integral to content learning.

It's also essential that you understand that effective use of technology as a learning tool requires a change in your own classroom behavior. Use of the word *facilitate* in this performance indicator is not accidental. As discussed in Performance Indicator II.E. (chapter 2), there's a time to offer direct instruction in technology skills and a time to expect students to apply these skills to complete academic activities. When progressing from teacher-led instruction to student-centered learning, you must make the shift from the role of classroom authority to provider of student support, encouraging students to assume increased responsibility for their own learning.

In this day of high-stakes testing and accountability, this may seem like a tall order. However, teachers who provide direct instruction in various learning strategies first, and then give students opportunities to apply them in a supervised setting, aren't wasting time during either phase. Rather, they're preparing students to become self-directed learners and problem solvers who aren't stymied by every challenge they meet.

This isn't a new concept. In his article "The WIRED Classroom," Jamie McKenzie wrote (1998, March):

> A good teacher knows when to act as Sage on the Stage and when to act as a Guide on the Side. Because student-centered learning can be time-consuming and messy, efficiency will sometimes argue for the Sage. When students are busy making up their own minds, the role of the teacher shifts. When questioning, problem solving and investigation become the priority classroom activities, the teacher becomes a Guide on the Side.

As you work toward making this transition, it's useful to conduct an occasional informal scan of the types of instructional strategies and learning activities used in the previous 4 weeks. How often were teacher-centered strategies employed? Were student-centered instructional strategies used? If so, how often? What kinds of activities did students engage in and what was their level of complexity?

It might be helpful to compare the activity objectives to the levels of Bloom's taxonomy, or a similar tool. Are the objectives spread across the continuum or clustered around the knowledge and comprehension levels?

The Internet hosts several Web sites that list the levels in Bloom's taxonomy and also provide descriptors. Here are three:

- Learning Skills Program—www.coun.uvic.ca/learn/program/hndouts/bloom.html
- Bloom's Taxonomy—www.kent.k12.wa.us/KSD/MA/resources/blooms/blooms.html
- The Taxonomy of Educational Objectives—www.humboldt.edu/~thal/bloomtax.html

The following table shows sample objectives for each level.

TABLE 3.1 ■ **Bloom's Taxonomy and lesson objectives**

TAXONOMY LEVEL	EXAMPLE OBJECTIVES Students will...
Knowledge	a. use a software program to create a timeline of events in the life of Abraham Lincoln. b. list the processes in the water cycle.
Comprehension	a. read *Abe Lincoln's Hat* by Martha Brenner and earn a passing score on the accompanying Accelerated Reader quiz. b. use a paint or draw program to create a flowchart showing the water cycle
Application	a. use presentation software to create an illustrated biography of Abraham Lincoln's life. b. build a model that simulates the water cycle.
Analysis	a. use concept mapping software to show similarities and differences between Abraham Lincoln and the current president. b. use a spreadsheet program to graph changes observed in the water cycle model.
Synthesis	a. use a wiki or online word processor to collaboratively write a one-act play about one event in Abraham Lincoln's life. b. devise a method to demonstrate transpiration in the water cycle model.
Evaluation	a. publish a booklet of the 5 most important things they learned about Abraham Lincoln and present it to the class, explaining their choices. b. explain why water is considered to be a "renewable resource."

You can quickly get a feel for classroom teaching and learning patterns by reviewing your lesson plan books using these questions about objectives, strategies, and activities. You can learn a lot simply by using three highlighters, one to mark teacher-centered lessons and activities, one for those that are student-centered, and the third to mark technology-supported activities. Use the results to determine whether there's a good balance among the three and if technology is being used appropriately.

Use the questions in table 3.2 to consider steps that might be taken to increase the facilitation of technology-enhanced experiences that address content standards and student technology standards.

TABLE 3.2 ■ **Performance Indicator III.A.**

Facilitate technology-enhanced experiences that address content standards and student technology standards.

Directions: Rate each numbered statement using the scale provided. Use the short answer areas to respond to prompts.

Rating Scale: **1** = Never **2** = Seldom **3** = Sometimes **4** = Often **5** = Regularly (as appropriate)					
1. I specifically reference academic standards in the lesson plans I write or use.	1	2	3	4	5
2. I specifically reference student technology standards in the technology-supported lesson plans I write or use.	1	2	3	4	5
3. I provide direct instruction in student technology skills.	1	2	3	4	5
4. Once technology skills are taught to my students, they're expected to apply those skills in academic activities.	1	2	3	4	5
The methods used to facilitate technology-enhanced experiences that address content standards and student technology standards include:					
List 2–3 steps you'll take to increase or improve facilitation of technology-enhanced experiences that address content standards and student technology standards:					

Using Technology to Address the Diverse Needs of Learners

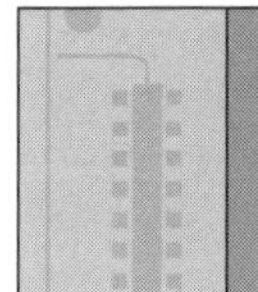

Performance Indicator III.B.

Use technology to support learner-centered strategies that address the diverse needs of students.

The use of technology to support the shift from predominately teacher-centered classrooms to learner-centered environments is an underlying theme that runs throughout the standards. This particular performance indicator specifically addresses this shift and raises the bar even higher by asking you to use these strategies to address the diverse needs of students. This means that occasional use of learner-centered strategies isn't enough. Rather, you must be familiar with and use a variety of learner-centered strategies, based on the diverse needs of your students.

The importance of student-centered instruction is based on two premises. First, learning is essentially an active endeavor. Confucius purportedly said, "I hear and I forget. I see and I remember. I do and I understand." Lecturing may be the cleanest way to document that prescribed material was covered. It may also be the easiest way to deal with a number of classroom management issues. But when it's the primary method of instruction, students lose out on many opportunities to become actively engaged in the learning process. With lectures, students hear and then tend to forget. A student-centered classroom encourages understanding through doing.

The second premise is that people learn in different ways, and it's your responsibility to address these diverse needs. The following statement is attributed to Dr. Rita Dunn of the Center for the Study of Learning and Teaching Styles at St. John's University: "If the child is not learning the way you are teaching, then you must teach in the way the child learns."

This sentiment flies in the face of a viewpoint still held by many educators that children need to adapt to the teacher's teaching style, not the other way around. This may have been true when one of the primary purposes of public education was to prepare students to work in manufacturing positions. However, the work world has changed. Today's students need skills that will help them work collaboratively using higher order thinking skills and problem-solving strategies.

This means that you need to create and support environments where students are active participants in their own learning. Just completing a directed task isn't enough; students must also have opportunities to engage in thought-provoking, meaningful work. You can expand or enhance a number of learner-centered strategies using technology. These strategies include:

- Reciprocal teaching: Designed to help students make sense of text, reciprocal teaching involves dialogue, either between students and teachers or among students, using four strategies: summarizing, question generating, clarifying, and predicting. Students and teachers take turns acting as the instructor.
- Cooperative learning: In this approach, students work on an assignment in small groups until all group members understand and complete the work.
- Project-based learning: This student-centered strategy emphasizes long-term, interdisciplinary activities based on real-world problems.
- Strategy instruction: This approach focuses on teaching students learning strategies along with concepts, emphasizing the importance of actively practicing these learning strategies.
- Inquiry-based learning: This approach encourages students to conduct research and use the information and data they find to construct meaning.

Remember that using technology to enable or enhance these kinds of activities requires that students have a good technology skill base and know how to use various technologies as tools for learning. You may predict, or even assign, specific uses of technology. For example, students can use technology for research, for online collaborative work, or for building a Web-based presentation. However, you should also be open to your students' ideas for using various technologies in new ways. For further reading on using technology to support learner-centered strategies that address the diverse needs of students, refer to chapter 2, Performance Indicators II.A. and II.B.

Addressing the needs of diverse learners also requires that you look for ways to adapt the use of existing technologies to support students with a variety of learning challenges. You should be familiar with commonly available assistive technologies. Performance Indicator VI.B. (chapter 6) provides a discussion of this topic. Teachers who are familiar with techniques that allow them to enlarge text, add narratives to files, and make use of hypertext to support divergent thinkers can couple these techniques with student-centered instructional strategies to provide additional support to children with special needs.

Use the statements in the following table to consider how you might increase the use of technology to support learner-centered strategies that address the diverse needs of students.

TABLE 3.2 ■ Performance Indicator III.B.

Use technology to support learner-centered strategies that address the diverse needs of students.

Directions: Rate each numbered statement using the scale provided. Use the short-answer areas to respond to prompts as appropriate.

Rating Scale: **1** = Never **2** = Seldom **3** = Sometimes **4** = Often **5** = Regularly (as appropriate)					
1. Technology is used to support learner-centered strategies that address the diverse needs of students.	1	2	3	4	5
List the learner-centered strategies used to support the diverse needs of students:					
Describe ways technology is used to enhance or expand use of the learner-centered strategies listed above:					
2. Special features of various technologies (e.g., enlarged text or narration) or other assistive technologies are used to support learner-centered strategies that address the diverse needs of students.	1	2	3	4	5
List 2–3 steps you will take to increase or improve the use of technology to support learner-centered strategies that address the diverse needs of students:					

Promoting Higher Order Thinking Skills and Creativity with Technology

Performance Indicator III.C.

Apply technology to develop students' higher order skills and creativity.

The findings of the Apple Classrooms of Tomorrow Project (1995) research, described in chapter 2, clearly show that technology use has the greatest impact on student performance when students engage in technology-supported activities at the appropriation and invention stages of use. Coincidentally, when working at these stages, students are often working collaboratively to complete a project or solve a problem, requiring use of higher order thinking skills and creativity in environments where technology is one of many available tools.

To meet Performance Indicator III.C., students must be provided opportunities to use technology tools to develop and strengthen their higher order thinking skills and creativity. If you want to increase your overall skills in developing curriculum to engage students' higher order thinking skills, you'll find good resources at:

- THE PRACTICE: An Emphasis on Thinking (The Knowledge Loom)— http://knowledgeloom.org/practice_basedoc.jsp?t=1&bpid=1205&aspect=1&location=2&parentid=1196&bpinterid=1196&spotlightid=1174
- Thinking Skills (Intel Innovation in Education)— www97.intel.com/en/ProjectDesign/ThinkingSkills/
- Topic: Student Learning (CARET)— http://caret.iste.org/index.cfm?fuseaction=evidence&answerID=7

In addition, a number of low- or no-cost software programs and Web-based tools can support this performance indicator. For example, programs published by Inspiration Software Inc. (Inspiration, Kidspiration, and InspireData) are designed to promote use of graphic organizers to stimulate critical thinking. Blogs (e.g., http://edublogs.org), wikis (e.g., http://pbwiki.com), and Webtop applications (e.g., www.thinkfree.com or www.writely.com) lend themselves well for use in higher order thinking activities.

Definitions

Weblog, or blog: Web sites comprised of dated postings in reverse chronological order. Blogs often focus on a specific topic and are written by one or more contributors. Postings usually include links to other Web sites and may also feature images. Some blogs allow readers to add their own comments.

Wiki: A collaborative Web site where content can be edited by anyone. Some wiki sites limit editing permission, using password protection or page locks.

Webtop applications: A Webtop application (e.g., word processor, spreadsheet, presentation program) that can be accessed from any Internet-connected computer. Files may be saved online as well, or downloaded to a computer or storage device. Webtop applications typically offer a collaboration feature: the original author of a file can invite others to view or edit the posted material.

Appropriation-stage activities look a lot like project-based learning (PBL). When engaged in PBL activities, students typically work in cooperative groups to complete a project designed by the teacher. The project must be well grounded in academic standards and is often a culminating activity designed to encourage students to apply skills and concepts learned through direct instruction. A major difference between PBL and more traditional projects is this direct tie to academic standards. Rather than being an add-on project completed at home or on Friday afternoons, PBL activities are an integral part of the instructional day. Existing projects can be expanded and enhanced using technology. You may either use the tools and reflections in chapter 2 to plan activities of this type or the online tools available on the Project-Based Learning site at http://pblchecklist.4teachers.org.

It's helpful to have access to models of students' use of technology tools to complete projects. You can review several excellent online resources for ideas, including:

- Apple Learning Interchange (http://ali.apple.com). This site offers such resources as Student Gallery, Lesson Ideas, and Technology Showcases.
- Edutopia (www.edutopia.org). The Magazine, Documentaries, and Multimedia sections of this site offer examples of best practices.
- Global Schoolnet (www.globalschoolnet.org/GSH/pr/). Current and past projects are showcased on this site.
- Baltimore County Public Schools' Office of Library Information Services (www.bcps.org/offices/lis/). The Information Literacy Process Model presented on this site is well worth checking out.

The WebQuest, an online inquiry-based model developed in 1995 by Bernie Dodge and Tom March, is a very popular appropriation-stage strategy among technology-using teachers. In a WebQuest, most or all of the information students interact with is accessed online. Videoconferencing is sometimes used to supplement text and graphics. Short-term WebQuests may be completed in 1–3 class sessions, while long-term WebQuests take 1–4 weeks to complete.

WebQuests consist of six elements: Introduction, Task, Information Sources, Process, Organizational Guidance, and Conclusion. Individuals might complete a WebQuest, but most are designed to be group activities. Hundreds of examples are posted on the Web. Bernie Dodge hosts the WebQuest News at http://Webquest.org. Another resource is the Saskatoon (East) School Division's WebQuest site, available at http://sesd.sk.ca/teacherresource/Webquest/Webquest.htm.

If you can't find an existing WebQuest that meets your needs, you'll want to consider using AT&T's Knowledge Network Explorer's free Filamentality tool at www.filamentality.com/wired/fil/. This tool offers several options for creating online student activities, including WebQuests. Once the WebQuest is created, AT&T Knowledge Ventures will host the activity for at least 1 year. To extend this time, simply edit the activity annually.

Invention-stage activities look a lot like constructivism, an instructional strategy that requires the learner to actively build understanding and knowledge. In this type of activity, the teacher poses a problem and asks students to identify and implement a strategy to solve the problem. The international ThinkQuest competition (www.thinkquest.org) is an excellent example of students' use of technology to solve problems. The ThinkQuest Library includes more than 5,500 examples of student work at this level.

You don't need templates for invention-stage activities. At this point, students should have enough experience using various technology tools that they can be expected to identify and use the appropriate tools. This could range from calculators, to computers, to digital cameras, and more. Peripherals such as probeware or scanners might be selected. All kinds of software or Web-based applications, including blogs, wikis, and podcasts, can be used at this level, depending on access and usefulness.

If you use technology at the appropriation and invention stages, you'll need to seek out like-minded colleagues in your grade level or department. On those occasions when implementation gets tricky, peer support goes a long way toward getting back on the right track. Also, when working collaboratively, you can share lesson plans and units—a big time saver for everyone!

Use the responses in the following table to consider steps you might take to apply technology to develop students' higher order thinking skills and creativity.

TABLE 3.4 ■ **Performance Indicator III.C.**

Apply technology to develop students' higher order skills and creativity.

Directions: Rate the numbered statement using the scale provided. Use the short-answer areas to respond to prompts or questions.

Rating Scale: **1** = Never **2** = Seldom **3** = Sometimes **4** = Often **5** = Regularly (as appropriate)					
1. I specifically plan opportunities for technology use that encourage development of students' higher order thinking skills and creativity.	1	2	3	4	5
The opportunities for technology use that encourage development of students' higher order thinking skills and creativity include:					
Which of the opportunities described are at the appropriation level and which are at the invention level? Explain your answer:					
Review at least three examples of student projects that use technology to encourage development of student's high order thinking skills and creativity. List the projects reviewed here: How could these projects be adapted for use in your classroom?					
List 2–3 steps you will take to increase or improve opportunities for technology use that encourage development of students' higher-order thinking skills and creativity:					

Managing the Technology-Enhanced Classroom

Performance Indicator III.D.

Manage student learning activities in a technology-enhanced environment.

The discussion of Performance Indicator II.E. in chapter 2 points out the need for teachers to plan strategies for managing student learning activities in a technology-enhanced environment. This performance indicator asks you to implement those plans.

This may not be as easy as you might think. It's one thing to come up with strategies in an empty classroom but quite another to stick to them when several students are clamoring for attention at the same time. The best-laid plans will fall by the wayside when you fail to take the time to explain procedures and hold students accountable for following them.

This is particularly true if you're unsure of your own technology skills. As pointed out before, the very first thing you need to do is take the time to teach new technology procedures before attempting to implement in a content-learning activity. It will save a great deal of time in the long run.

There's a second strategy you can use to help ensure a smooth implementation of technology: supervise, supervise, supervise! Theoretically, Internet filters block objectionable Web sites and prohibited activities, such as chat rooms. However, filters are not foolproof. Also, theoretically, students and their parents understand all the provisions of an Acceptable Use Policy (AUP) when they sign it. However, these documents are often written in incomprehensible legalese and are quickly forgotten. Students may attempt to install unapproved programs or files on a school computer, use someone else's password to access the network, or find themselves in awkward online situations either accidentally or by design.

It's your job to review acceptable behavior with students and actively monitor their activity. This can often be handled with simple strategies such as being highly visible, placing the classroom printer next to the teacher station, or making students accountable for turning in some type of artifact when they finish the day's work. For further reading on how to effectively monitor student use of technology, refer to chapter 6, Performance Indicator VI.A.

Another argument for careful monitoring is the need to maintain flexibility in grouping and assignments. Just as in more traditional learning environments, sometimes teachers or students need to fall back on a "Plan B." Teachers who are aware of what's happening in the classroom can step in to help students regroup or suggest a different learning strategy if unanticipated problems arise.

Use the questions in the following table to consider steps that you might take to manage student learning activities in a technology-enhanced environment.

TABLE 3.5 ■ **Performance Indicator III.D.**

III.D. Manage student learning activities in a technology-enhanced environment.

Directions: Give a Yes or No answer to questions 1 and 2. Use the short-answer areas to elaborate on your answers.

Question	Yes	No
1. Do you have a specific plan for managing student learning activities in a technology-enhanced environment?		
2. If so, have you actually implemented this plan?		
If you've implemented your plan, describe what is or is not working well. If you haven't implemented the plan, explain why:		
List 2–3 steps you'll take to improve your plan for managing student learning activities in a technology-enhanced environment:		

Action Plan

Now that you've read about each performance indicator for Standard III and have had the opportunity to think about your level of implementation for each indicator, it's time to develop an action plan to improve or expand your professional practice in this area.

First, review your responses to the statements and questions in each performance indicator table. It's not possible to master every performance indicator at once, so choose one at a time. Build your plan using the steps that you identified you might take for the chosen performance indicator and complete your action plan by using the table below. Performance Indicator III.C. has been used as a sample.

TABLE 3.6 ■ **Teachers implement curriculum plans that include methods and strategies for applying technology to maximize student learning**

Performance Indicator	Next Steps	I need to work on this step with the following people...	I will know this step has been achieved when...	Timeline
III.C. Apply technology to develop students' higher order skills and creativity.	*Use a wiki to encourage student collaboration and showcase student work for the semester project.*	*Teachers in my department, district IT staff.*	*The project is completed and student work is posted on the wiki.*	*End of the semester.*
	1.			
	2.			
	3.			

Resources

ARTICLES AND REPORTS

Apple Classrooms of Tomorrow Project. (1995). ACOT's *10 Year Report.* [Online report]. Available: www.apple.com/education/k12/leadership/acot/library.html

Glamser, Mari Clayton. (1998, April 19). *Notes from a teacher/soldier in the learning revolution.* [Online article]. Available: www.middleWeb.com/StdCtrdTchng.html

McKenzie, Jamie. (1998, March). *The WIRED Classroom.* [Online article]. Available: http://fno.org/mar98/flotilla2.html

North Central Regional Educational Laboratory. *Focus on student-centered learning.* [Online handbook]. Available: www.ncrel.org/tplan/handbook/foc.htm

WEB SITES

Apple Learning Interchange. Available: http://ali.apple.com

AT&T Knowledge Network Explorer's Blue Web'N. Available: www.filamentality.com/wired/bluewebn/

AT&T Knowledge Network Explorer's Filamentality. Available: www.filamentality.com/wired/fil/index.html

Baltimore County Public Schools' Office of Library Information Services. Available: www.bcps.org/offices/lis/

Center for Applied Research in Educational Technology, Topic: Student Learning. Available: http://caret.iste.org/index.cfm?fuseaction=evidence&answerID=7

The Education Alliance at Brown University, The Knowledge Loom. Available: http://knowledgeloom.org

Edutopia. Available: www.edutopia.org

Global Schoolnet. Available: www.globalschoolnet.org/GSH/pr/

Intel Innovation in Education, Thinking Skills. Available: www97.intel.com/en/ProjectDesign/ThinkingSkills/

Project Based Learning. Available: http://pblchecklist.4teachers.org

Saskatoon (East) School Division's WebQuest site. Available: http://sesd.sk.ca/teacherresource/Webquest/Webquest.htm

ThinkQuest. Available: www.thinkquest.org

University of Victoria Counselling Services, *Bloom's Taxonomy.* Available: www.coun.uvic.ca/learn/program/hndouts/bloom.html

WebQuest News. Available: http://Webquest.org

Chapter 4

STANDARD IV

Assessment and Evaluation

Teachers apply technology to facilitate a variety of effective assessment and evaluation strategies.

PERFORMANCE INDICATORS FOR TEACHERS

IV.A. Apply technology in assessing student learning of subject matter using a variety of assessment techniques.

IV.B. Use technology resources to collect and analyze data, interpret results, and communicate findings to improve instructional practice and maximize student learning.

IV.C. Apply multiple methods of evaluation to determine students' appropriate use of technology resources for learning, communication, and productivity.

Chapter 4 Overview

Good thoughts are no better than good dreams, unless they be executed.
—RALPH WALDO EMERSON

What gets measured gets done.
—TOM PETERS

Taken together, these two quotes underscore the importance of assessment and evaluation in education. A well-designed assessment plan enables you to identify strengths and weaknesses in the instructional program as well as students' mastery of concepts. Unfortunately, much of the assessment that takes place happens after the fact, when it's too late to repeat your instructional process or change direction.

Standard IV encourages teachers to use technology tools to implement assessment strategies that measure the impact of instruction and student learning throughout the instructional process, and then use the data to make immediate improvements and adjustments.

At first reading, Performance Indicators IV.A. and IV.B. appear to be nearly identical, but there is a difference. Performance Indicator IV.A. points out the importance of using technology to support a variety of assessment techniques for all content areas. This entails assessment planning that incorporates the use of technology tools for developing assessment instruments. Performance Indicator IV.B. focuses on using technology to collect, analyze, interpret, and communicate assessment information, as well as to implement the assessment plan in all content areas.

Performance Indicator IV.C. is the only one of the three that specifically addresses measuring students' proficiency in using technology as a learning tool. This performance indicator is receiving more attention now that No Child Left Behind requirements include the assessment of all eighth-graders' technology literacy. However, it's important to remember that this is just one part of Standard IV.

Using Technology to Assess Learning

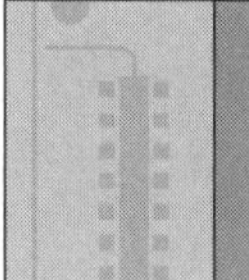

Performance Indicator IV.A.

Apply technology in assessing student learning of subject matter using a variety of assessment techniques.

Effective assessment of student learning requires thoughtful planning. A comprehensive classroom assessment plan incorporates three kinds of assessment: diagnostic, formative, and summative. Diagnostic assessments are administered before instruction begins in order to identify students' knowledge and skill level as well as their academic strengths and weaknesses. Formative assessments may be informal and often aren't graded. Used throughout instruction, these assessments provide a vehicle for monitoring student progress and making adjustments in instructional delivery. Summative assessments often take the form of a large project or test administered at the end of an instructional unit, semester, or school year. They're used to measure what the student has learned.

All of this takes time, and educators are increasingly concerned about over-assessing students. As a result, teachers tend to rely most heavily on summative assessment. You may incorporate some diagnostic assessment, but many teachers make little regular use of formal formative assessment. It's possible, however, to incorporate comprehensive assessment into the instructional day without overburdening teachers or students, particularly when various technology tools are used to develop and implement the assessments.

Developing an Assessment Plan

The assessment plan will dictate when it's appropriate to use technology-supported tools for monitoring and evaluation, not the other way around. Consequently, it's important to begin by developing the plan. Ask yourself the following questions:

- What types of assessment will be used throughout the school year?
- What purpose will be served by each assessment?
- What kinds of assessment tools will provide the necessary information in the most reliable and least labor-intensive manner?

Use a calendar to block out instructional units and map the assessment strategies to be used throughout the year for diagnosis, monitoring, and final assessment. Adjustments will need to be made as the school year progresses; however, preplanning helps assure that balanced, regular assessment occurs in all three areas. An electronic calendar can be used for initial planning, making it easier to make changes as needed. Many teachers are familiar with Outlook (http://office.microsoft.com/outlook/) or the calendars available on handheld computers and smartphones. Free Web-based calendars can also be used effectively, such as Yahoo! (www.calendar.yahoo.com), 30Boxes (http://30boxes.com), and AirSet (www.airset.com). Teachers working in teams can use features that enable them to share their electronic calendars with other team members so that the assessment plan can be developed collaboratively.

Don't be surprised that it's easiest to plug in summative assessments. Weekly tests, chapter tests, major projects, and midterm and end-of-year exams are a snap to identify and schedule. Opportunities for diagnostic assessment also occur frequently throughout the school year, and appropriate times for certain types of diagnostic assessments are easily predicted. For example, content pretests can be scheduled at the beginning of a chapter or instructional unit.

However, other diagnostic tools should also be used during the school year. They provide important information that wouldn't be captured otherwise. For example, it's very helpful to take a little time early in the school year to gather data about students' interests and preferred learning styles. Block out some time for this type of diagnostic assessment. If the district doesn't have an adopted interest inventory or learning styles assessment in place, many examples are available on the Web.

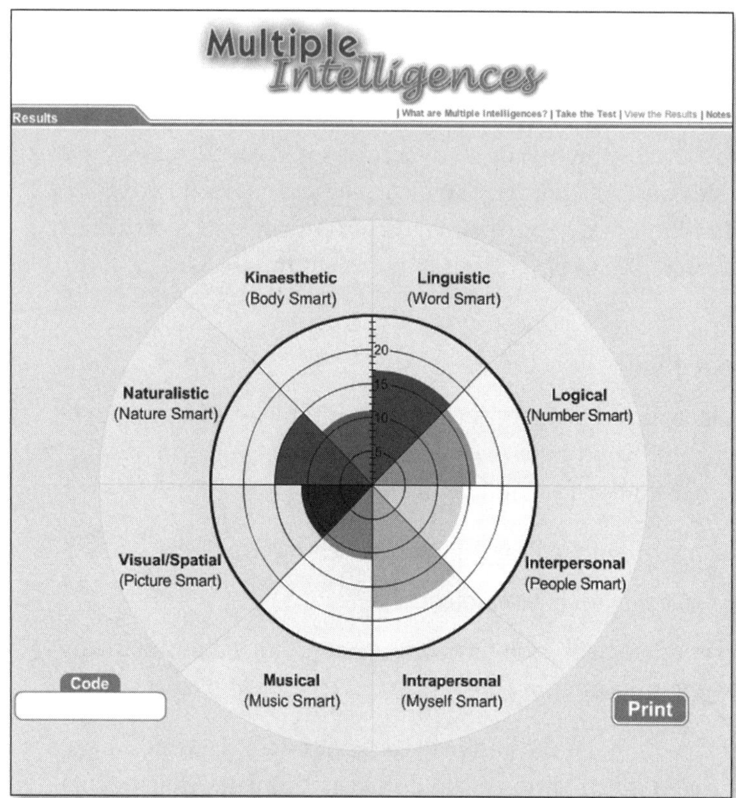

FIGURE 4.1 The printable response graph generated by the Birmingham Grid for Learning (BGfL) Multiple Intelligences Wheel provides teachers and students a quick snapshot of dominant intelligences.

The most challenging task will be to identify when and how to use formative assessments. Formative assessments enable you to make certain that instructional goals are being accomplished and that students are engaged in their learning. Formative assessment takes many shapes: teacher observation, quizzes, homework assignments, and informal student surveys, to name just a few. You unconsciously conduct a formative assessment every time you gauge the impact of an instructional approach based on a student's response to a lesson. A more formalized assessment requires clear documentation over time. Take the time to consider appropriate formative assessment strategies that can be used on a regular basis, and add these to the plan.

Before identifying technology tools that might be used to develop assessment instruments, review the type and frequency of assessments listed on the calendar. Ask yourself these questions:

- Is there a good balance?
- Is the purpose for each assessment clear?
- Will the assessment yield information that can be used to improve instruction?

When the answer to each question is yes, it's time to consider how technology can be used to facilitate the creation of assessment tools.

Using Technology to Create Assessment Tools

Begin by making a list of existing assessment tools. How many of these tools are supported by technology? For example, most textbook series now offer technology-based supplemental materials, including diagnostic and summative assessments. Has the district purchased these optional software programs or online subscriptions? What other technology-supported supplemental programs are available? This includes programs such as Accelerated Reader, Reading Counts, Accelerated Math, and so forth. Which of these resources can either be used as is or adapted for specific student needs?

When no technology-based supplemental materials are available, you can use several different kinds of technology tools to create your own assessment instruments. If it's necessary to take this route, there are steps to take and resources that can be used. For example, take stock of your and your students' access to various technologies, the quality of the school's infrastructure, and the speed of the school's online connection. In situations where teachers have ready access but students don't, you might confine technology use to such management tasks related to assessment as creating instruments, inputting and analyzing data, and reporting results. In cases where students have ready access to technology, it's possible to automate the actual administration of the assessment as well.

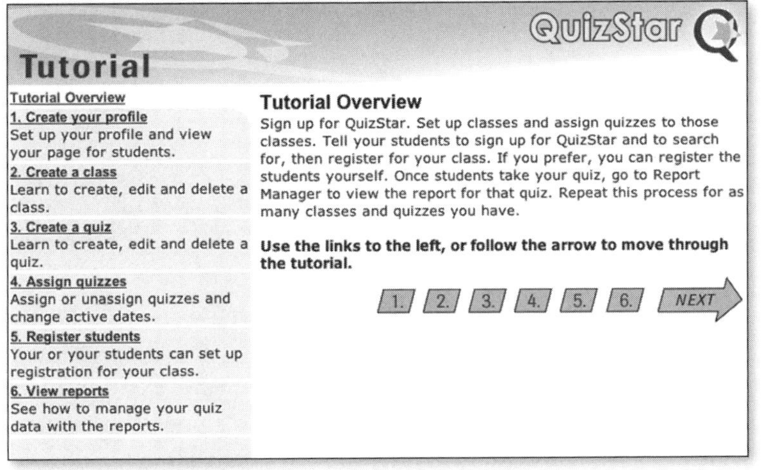

FIGURE 4.2 QuizStar's easy-to-use tutorial enables teachers to begin creating quizzes in just minutes.

Teachers often begin by using online quiz and test generators to develop objective diagnostic or summative quizzes and tests. You can find a number of free and low-cost online options for completing this task. For example:

- Easy Test Maker—www.easytestmaker.com
- QuizStar—http://quizstar.4teachers.org
- Quiz Center—http://school.discovery.com/quizcenter/quizcenter.html
- Quia—www.quia.com

Some of these tools also allow students to complete quizzes and tests online. In these cases, the completed tests are scored online, and then simple reports are available to the teacher. When taking a test online isn't an option due to limitations of the Web site or lack of student access to technology, you can save and print the test, then administer and grade it in the traditional way.

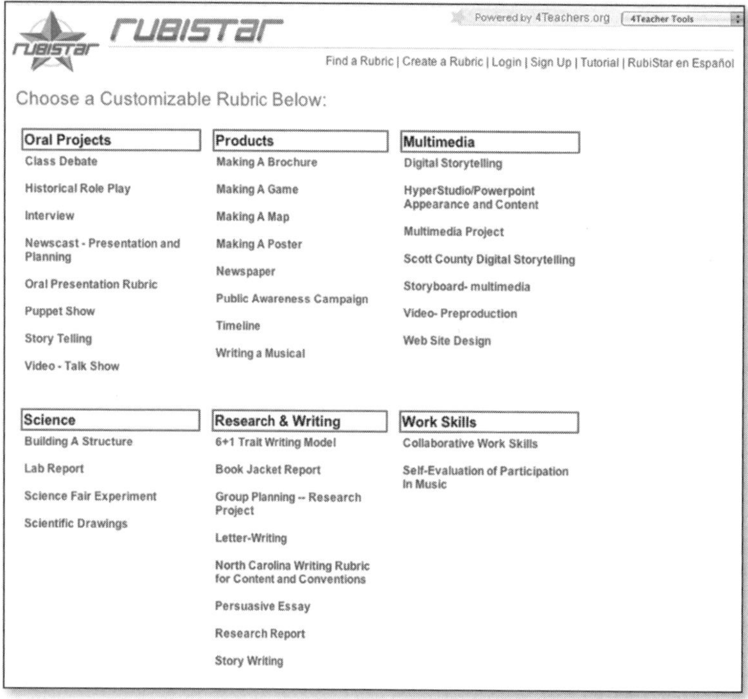

FIGURE 4.3 On the RubiStar site, you can either choose from dozens of customizable rubrics or create your own from scratch.

Rubrics are a popular assessment tool, but not all teachers have a great deal of experience in designing them. You can find free online tools that provide templates to guide you through the process of developing a rubric. These sites may also offer libraries of existing templates for teacher use. Once the rubric is created, you can save and print it for classroom use. Here are two examples of online rubric builders:

- RubiStar—http://rubistar.4teachers.org
- Rubric Builder—http://landmark-project.com/classWeb/tools/rubric_builder.php

A word processor can be used to create assessment tools as well. In addition to the obvious ability to type and print quizzes, tests, rubrics, and so forth, Microsoft Word has features that enable users to create forms that can be completed either on- or off-line. This is especially handy when you want to create formative observation tools such as checklists, or forms that include places for anecdotal notes. These forms can then be completed on the fly, using a laptop or tablet computer.

Programs are also available for teachers who want to create forms on a computer and transfer them to handheld computers, for even greater mobility. A few examples include Software HanDBase (DDH Software, www.ddhsoftware.com/forms.html), Documents to Go (DataViz, www.dataviz.com/products/documentstogo/), and FileMaker Mobile 8 (FileMaker, Inc., www.filemaker.com/products/fmm/). Forms of this type are especially useful when conducting observations outdoors or when it's necessary to move around the classroom during the observation.

Student surveys designed to obtain feedback about learning experiences are another kind of formative assessment. You can use several Web-based tools and software programs to survey students. Two online survey generators, Zoomerang (www.zoomerang.com) and SurveyMonkey (www.surveymonkey.com), offer limited free subscriptions. A third online service, ProfilerPRO (http://profilerpro.com), is free to educators, but it's more challenging to master initially. Any of these survey generators can be used to create and deploy simple student surveys. The sites also tabulate results and make reports available, depending on the type of subscription held by the creator of the survey. You can also use blogs to gather student feedback by posting a prompt and asking students to reply. These responses are more difficult to tabulate, but they still provide valuable information.

Some commercial products also enhance classroom assessment. Grade book programs, spreadsheets, and databases are classic examples. If you use assessments such as Running Records or DIBELS to monitor students' reading progress, you can use specially designed programs for handheld computers from companies such as Wireless Generation (www.wirelessgeneration.com/Web/). If you teach in districts where standards-based student profiles must be maintained, you might be interested in a program such as Learner Profile 3.0 (www.learnerprofile.com). This software enables you to customize forms to include the specific objectives and performance indicators tracked in the district's student profiles.

Personal response systems are growing in popularity as tools for conducting quick diagnostic quizzes and checking for understanding throughout a lesson. Each student uses a remote-control device to select an answer to an objective question projected on a screen. The infrared remote controls communicate with a computer running software that tabulates the responses. In most cases, each remote control has a specific identifying number. This allows you to track individual student responses as well as the group aggregate. Examples include InterWrite PRS (GTCO CalComp, www.gtcocalcomp.com), Beyond Question (Smartroom Learning Solutions, www.smartroom.com), and CPSrf (eInstruction, http://einstruction.com).

Electronic portfolios are also garnering a great deal of attention. If you're interested in automating student portfolios, you may want to begin with the KEEP Toolkit (www.cfkeep.org/static/index.html), a free resource from the Carnegie Foundation. Some teachers are also experimenting with the use of blogs and wikis for developing electronic portfolios. Actual examples of K–12 student work are difficult to cite due to privacy concerns. You can get a sense of how blogs and wikis work in e-portfolios by visiting the More Examples page of the myEport.com site (www.myeport.com/published/t/es/test/home/2/) or by visiting the Blogs and Wikis for ePortfolios page hosted by the University of Southern California's Center for Scholarly Technology at www.usc.edu/programs/cst/tls/pilot/blogsandwikis.html.

Integrated learning systems and computer-assisted instruction programs are not discussed here for two reasons. First, these are large-scale purchases. If a district doesn't have a system of this type in place, an individual classroom teacher will not make this kind of purchase. Second, when teachers have access to this type of system, usage mandates or controls are usually already in place.

Use the following table to identify ways you might apply technology in assessing student learning of subject matter using a variety of assessment techniques.

TABLE 4.1 ■ **Performance Indicator IV.A.**

Apply technology in assessing student learning of subject matter using a variety of assessment techniques.

Directions: Rate each numbered statement using the scale provided. Use the short-answer areas to respond to prompts.

Rating Scale: **1** = Never **2** = Seldom **3** = Sometimes **4** = Often **5** = Regularly (as appropriate)					
1. I develop a specific assessment plan for the academic year.	1	2	3	4	5
2. I specifically plan and use diagnostic assessments with my students.	1	2	3	4	5
3. I specifically plan and use formative assessments with my students.	1	2	3	4	5
4. I specifically plan and use summative assessments with my students.	1	2	3	4	5
The methods I use to apply technology in assessing student learning of subject matter using a variety of assessment techniques include:					
List 2–3 steps you will take to increase or improve application of technology in assessing student learning of subject matter using a variety of assessment techniques:					

Collecting and Using Data to Improve Instruction and Learning

Performance Indicator IV.B.

Use technology resources to collect and analyze data, interpret results, and communicate findings to improve instructional practice and maximize student learning.

At one time, the teacher's primary data collection tool was a grade book. Scores for homework, class assignments, quizzes, tests, and projects were recorded. Between grading periods, the primary use of the data was to identify students who hadn't turned in assignments.

When standardized test scores gained prominence as an assessment tool, teachers and administrators began to pay more attention to the annual testing reports that accompanied the reports of individual student scores. But they tended to focus on aggregate scores for grade levels rather than individual student reports, largely because by the time they received the test scores, the school year was over and students had moved on. Some districts also asked teachers to keep individual student profiles that documented whether students had mastered discrete skill sets. These profiles and test scores were filed in students' cumulative record folders, but teachers rarely used this information later for diagnosis or formative assessment.

In large part, educators made infrequent use of the data they collected because they had no easy way to manipulate and analyze the data. Advances in technology have changed that. Most teachers now have access to computers and software for data entry, analysis, and reporting. Most districts now receive standardized test data in electronic format, which makes it possible to disaggregate the data in almost any way imaginable.

What options are available and how can you use these tools to improve instructional practice and maximize student learning? The following discussion explores ways you can collect and analyze data, then interpret and share results to maximize student learning.

Data Collection and Analysis

You often start off using a grade book program or spreadsheet to track student grades. Even though data entry still takes time, these tools are attractive, because once the scores are entered, it's possible to calculate grades in a fraction of the time it used to take.

Grade book programs often include reporting options that can be used to analyze trends in student performance. Spreadsheets offer a variety of data analysis and reporting options, too. Districts that have adopted a Student Information System (SIS) may offer online grading to teachers, as well as options for generating multiple reports.

Online quizzes and tests are growing in popularity, as districts increase student access to computers and high speed Internet connections. Many textbook publishers now offer online testing options, and you can use various Web sites to write and administer your own quizzes and tests (see the resources section for more information).

One of the biggest attractions of online testing is that results are available almost immediately. Although this works best for assessments with objective items, Web-based solutions can score a variety of short-answer questions, even essays.

Other tools for data collection and analysis are also available. The discussion of Performance Indicator IV.A. earlier in chapter 4 mentions having student interest inventories and learning style assessments in place. Most of the learning style assessments listed in this chapter's resources section are administered online and include simple reports that students may print out for future reference.

You can gather many types of data using a handheld computer and special software. By synchronizing the data to a computer, various reports can be generated. Student surveys conducted online are automatically tabulated, and the results can usually be exported into a spreadsheet program for further analysis. In addition, electronic portfolios make tracking samples of student work over a period of years manageable.

The district SIS is also a source of useful data for classroom teachers. Typically, a system of this type is used to track student attendance, individual standardized test scores, discipline records, health information, and more. Some districts provide teachers direct access to certain student reports available through the system. Others require that you request the reports. In either case, it's worth taking the time to access this information, because it can be used to develop a deeper understanding of each student.

Examples of Interest Inventories and Learning Style Assessments

Interest Inventories

Interest Inventory WebQuest: http://faculty.citadel.edu/hewett/web_files/interestweb.html

The Learner–Interests: www.saskschools.ca/curr_content/adapthandbook/learner/interest.html

Learning Style Assessments

Birmingham Grid for Learning (BGfL) Multiple Intelligences Wheel: www.bgfl.org/multipleintelligences/

FCPSTeach.org's Interest and Learning Profile Inventories: www.fcpsteach.org/gt_renzulli/

Multiple Intelligence Test for Children: www.mitest.com/omitest.htm

Seven Intelligences Checklist–Youth Version: www.mitest.com/o2ndary.htm

Interpreting Results to Improve Instructional Practice and Maximize Student Learning

Access to data and reports means very little if the results aren't interpreted, communicated, and used to improve classroom experiences and support student learning. Unfortunately, assessment results are often filed away without being reviewed, even when technology tools have been used to generate reports that are easy to read and interpret.

Diagnostic assessment results can be used to decide what material needs to be covered during instruction. It can help teachers organize flexible learning groups. Formative assessments, such as grades for homework and class work, quiz scores, and teacher observations, provide a vehicle for monitoring student progress and making immediate adjustments in instructional strategies when needed. In the short term, summative assessment results identify those students who need to spend more time studying one or more concepts before moving on. In the long term, these results provide a global view of programs and student performance that can be used to evaluate strengths and weaknesses of both.

A word of caution: data interpretation requires training and takes practice. It's important to view the data in context. A sharp increase in absenteeism during a flu epidemic means something completely different than a similar absentee rate just before the holiday season. A list of averaged scores doesn't provide the same information as a report on the percentage of students who demonstrate mastery of a concept. Standardized test score results are often misinterpreted due to a lack of understanding of national percentile rankings or grade-level equivalencies. Many teachers find that it's helpful to review data with colleagues in Reflective Practice Groups (RPGs), particularly when it appears that a major change is indicated (see next section).

What Is a Reflective Practice Group?

Reflective Practice Groups (RPGs) make it possible for individual teachers to interact with colleagues to share experiences and identify new approaches to problem solving. The most effective groups cross grade levels and content areas. RPGs typically involve educators with various levels of teaching experience and include site administrators. These groups meet at least monthly to discuss challenges and to evaluate the impact of members' teaching practices. Discussions are confidential and aren't tied to performance evaluation.

Sharing Results to Improve Instructional Practice and Maximize Student Learning

Who needs to be made aware of assessment results? As mentioned above, teachers benefit from examining results in RPGs. This can be helpful in interpreting results, but it also provides a venue for colleagues to discuss strategies for improving instruction and maximizing student learning. Teaching is definitely a profession where collective wisdom strengthens individual practice and can lead to systemic reform.

Parents also need to be kept apprised of student progress. Traditional formats for sharing this information include report cards, school accountability reports, individual standardized test reports, and so forth. Technology tools that facilitate communication between home and school include school and classroom Web sites—where school and district reports are made available to parents and community members—and password-protected Web sites—where teachers can post grade reports for parents and students to access on an individual basis. A growing number of teachers are also using blogs to post weekly informational updates, homework assignments, and other information for parents.

There's an important caveat for teachers, however. Many parents now want to use e-mail for home to school communication. E-mail is a good tool to use for general information or to set an appointment, but sensitive student information needs to be discussed in a face-to-face meeting, not through e-mail. There are at least two reasons for this. First, e-mail isn't 100% secure and can be accessed by individuals other than the addressee. Second, some parent-teacher conferences are emotional events. Without the visual and aural cues provided in a face-to-face meeting, it's too easy to misconstrue remarks made, leading to increased problems.

Use the following table to identify ways you might use technology resources to collect and analyze data, interpret results, and communicate findings to improve instructional practice and maximize student learning.

TABLE 4.2 ■ Performance Indicator IV.B.

Use technology resources to collect and analyze data, interpret results, and communicate findings to improve instructional practice and maximize student learning.

Directions: Rate each numbered statement using the scale provided. Use the short-answer areas to respond to prompts.

Rating Scale: **1** = Never **2** = Seldom **3** = Sometimes **4** = Often **5** = Regularly (as appropriate)					
1. I use online tools to administer student assessments.	1	2	3	4	5
Explain your response:					
2. I use technology-supported tools to collect and analyze data.	1	2	3	4	5
Explain your response:					
3. I use reports generated with technology-supported tools to interpret assessment results.	1	2	3	4	5
Explain your response:					

(Continued)

TABLE 4.2 ■ **Performance Indicator IV.B.** *(Continued)*

4. I use technology-supported tools to share assessment results with colleagues and parents.	1	2	3	4	5
Explain your response:					
List 2–3 steps you will take to increase or improve use of technology resources to collect and analyze data, interpret results, and communicate findings to improve instructional practice and maximize student learning:					

Assessing Students' Technology Literacy

Performance Indicator IV.C.

Apply multiple methods of evaluation to determine students' appropriate use of technology resources for learning, communication, and productivity.

School districts that accept certain federal funding are now required to measure students' technology proficiency by the end of eighth grade. Nearly every state in the union has adopted or adapted the National Educational Technology Standards for Students (NETS•S) as its framework for defining appropriate student use of technology resources. In addition, many states' content frameworks include references to technology use.

In response to federal requirements to measure students' technology proficiency, most districts have developed a scope and sequence chart or list of competencies for student technology skills that are based on NETS•S performance indicators and other state documents. Therefore, how and when you assess student use of technology resources may be mandated by these recent developments. Examples of competencies are available at the Student Technology Literacy Proficiency Checklist Web site (www.aea8.k12.ia.us/documents/u_031404213821.pdf) and the Technology Competencies and Standards Web site (www.tcet.unt.edu/START/assess/standard.htm).

The first step in assessing students' use of technology resources is to become familiar with the district plan. Here are a few questions to consider:

- Does the district's plan treat this as a separate assessment, or is assessment of technology skills embedded in content area assessments?
- Are expectations defined by grade level or by grade-level clusters (e.g., PK–2, 3–5, 6–8, 9–12)?
- Does the assessment focus just on personal productivity, or are information literacy and problem-solving strategies also assessed?
- What assessment instruments are provided (e.g., checklists, rubrics, self-assessments)?

Next, determine how this plan will be interwoven into daily classroom practice. If the district plan embeds assessment of technology skills within content area activities, the alignment should be readily apparent. But if this isn't the case, it will be necessary to examine the technology competencies and ensure that opportunities for assessment are built into the individual classroom assessment plan. If you're meeting the performance indicators for Standards II and III, you'll have little difficulty including the assessment piece, because the technology-supported instruction and activities that lay the foundation for this assessment will already be in place.

Finally, make sure the classroom assessment plan includes diagnostic, formative, and summative assessments of student technology use. The district plan may already include various assessments. If not, a number of online resources provide examples of different ways to measure proficiency in these areas. For example, the NETS Online Technology Assessment (www.iste.org/inhouse/resources/asmt/msiste/), developed by the Microsoft Corporation and ISTE, includes 12 activities for eighth-grade students that embed technology skills in activities designed to complete a project or solve a problem. The resources section at the end of this chapter lists Web sites that include sample checklists and rubrics for measuring students' technology proficiency.

Use the following table to identify ways you might apply multiple methods of evaluation to determine students' appropriate use of technology resources for learning, communication, and productivity.

TABLE 4.3 ■ Performance Indicator IV.C.

Apply multiple methods of evaluation to determine students' appropriate use of technology resources for learning, communication, and productivity.

Directions: Rate each numbered statement using the scale provided. Use the short-answer areas to respond to prompts.

Rating Scale: **1** = Never **2** = Seldom **3** = Sometimes **4** = Often **5** = Regularly (as appropriate)					
1. I use multiple methods of evaluation to determine students' appropriate use of technology resources for learning.	1	2	3	4	5
Explain your answer:					
2. I use multiple methods of evaluation to determine students' appropriate use of technology resources for communication.	1	2	3	4	5
Explain your answer:					
3. I use multiple methods of evaluation to determine students' appropriate use of technology resources for productivity.	1	2	3	4	5
Explain your answer:					
List 2–3 steps you'll take to increase or improve use of multiple methods of evaluation to determine students' appropriate use of technology resources for learning, communication, and productivity:					

Action Plan

Now that you've read about each performance indicator for Standard IV and have had the opportunity to think about your level of implementation for each indicator, it's time to develop an action plan to improve or expand your professional practice in this area.

Review your responses to the statements and questions in each performance indicator table. It's not possible to master every performance indicator at once, so choose one at a time. Build your plan using the steps you identified you might take for the chosen performance indicator and complete your action plan by using the table below. Performance Indicator IV.A. has been used as a sample.

TABLE 4.4 ▪ **Teachers apply technology to facilitate a variety of effective assessment and evaluation strategies**

Performance Indicator	Next Steps	I need to work on this step with the following people...	I will know this step has been achieved when...	Timeline
IV.A. Apply technology in assessing student learning of subject matter using a variety of assessments.	*Poll other teachers in my grade-level cluster to find out what diagnostic assessment they use, and collect samples.*	*All teachers of Grades 3–5 at my site (and possibly teachers at nearby schools).*	*I have poll results and sample assessments I can review and discuss with fellow grade-level cluster teachers.*	*End of first quarter.*
	1.			
	2.			
	3.			

Resources

ARTICLES AND REPORTS

SETDA, National Leadership Institute's Toolkit 2005: *Evaluation of Student Achievement.* Available: www.setda.org/Toolkit2004/evaluation_01_chapter_summary.htm

INTEREST INVENTORIES

Interest Inventory WebQuest.
Available: http://faculty.citadel.edu/hewett/Web_files/interestWeb.html

The Learner–Interests.
Available: www.saskschools.ca/curr_content/adapthandbook/learner/interest.html

LEARNING STYLE ASSESSMENTS

Birmingham Grid for Learning (BGfL) Multiple Intelligences Wheel.
Available: www.bgfl.org/multipleintelligences/

FCPSTeach.org's Interest and Learning Profile Inventories.
Available: www.fcpsteach.org/gt_renzulli/

Multiple Intelligence Test for Children. Available: www.mitest.com/omitest.htm

Seven Intelligences Checklist: Youth Version. Available: www.mitest.com/o2ndary.htm

RUBRIC BUILDERS

RubiStar. Available: http://rubistar.4teachers.org

Rubric Builder. Available: http://landmark-project.com/classWeb/tools/rubric_builder.php

TEST GENERATORS

East Test Maker. Available: www.easytestmaker.com

Quia. Available: www.quia.com

Quiz Center. Available: http://school.discovery.com/quizcenter/quizcenter.html

QuizStar. Available: http://quizstar.4teachers.org

WEB SITES

Addison Central Supervisory Union Information Technology Assessment Rubrics: Profiles of Technology Literate Students. Available: www.acsu.k12.vt.us/assessment/

Guidelines for Rubric Development.
Available: http://edWeb.sdsu.edu/triton/july/rubrics/Rubric_Guidelines.html

MyEport.com ePortfolio. More Examples.
Available: www.myeport.com/published/t/es/test/home/2/

National Center for Educational Accountability: *Use Data to Inform Instruction.* Available: www.just4kids.org/bestpractice/practice_definition.fm?sub=State&study=Washington&detailid=75

National Educational Technology Standards. Available: www.iste.org/NETS

Pre-K–12 Technology Scope and Sequence. Available: www.my-ecoach.com/scope/intro.html

Student Technology Literacy Proficiency Checklist.
Available: www.aea8.k12.ia.us/documents/u_031404213821.pdf

Technology Competencies and Standards.
Available: www.tcet.unt.edu/START/assess/standard.htm

University of Southern California's Center for Scholarly Technology. Blogs and Wikis for Collaboration and ePortfolios.
Available: www.usc.edu/programs/cst/tls/pilot/blogsandwikis.html

Using Data to Improve Student Achievement. Available: www.mdk12.org/data/course/

Chapter 5

STANDARD V

Productivity and Professional Practice

Teachers use technology to enhance their productivity and professional practice.

PERFORMANCE INDICATORS FOR TEACHERS

V.A. Use technology resources to engage in ongoing professional development and lifelong learning.

V.B. Continually evaluate and reflect on professional practice to make informed decisions regarding the use of technology in support of student learning.

V.C. Apply technology to increase productivity.

V.D. Use technology to communicate and collaborate with peers, parents, and the larger community in order to nurture student learning.

Chapter 5 Overview

As recently as one generation ago, most workers (including educators) could complete a formal course of training in a particular skill or profession and be well prepared for a lifetime career. While periodic updates and recertification training may have been required, this was typically designed to supplement the individual's existing skill set.

The emergence of the information age, however, has dramatically shortened the time it takes for work skills to become outdated. In their book *Finding and Keeping Great Employees*, Harris and Brannick (1999) estimate that today it takes just 30 to 36 months for one-half of a worker's skills to become obsolete. Teachers who feel overwhelmed by system-wide changes and the increasing number of demands placed on them are experiencing this firsthand.

The performance indicators for this standard focus on teachers' use of technology for their own professional growth and practice. Teachers who engage in technology-supported professional development; reflect on the impact of their use of technology; use technology themselves in daily activities; and take advantage of technologies that enable them to communicate and collaborate in new, powerful ways are more likely to make effective use of technology with students than those who don't personally use technology. What's more, they're likely to do a better job in general because they make more efficient use of their time. For many teachers, however, meeting these performance indicators requires fundamental changes in their attitudes about professional development and how they conduct daily business.

Integrating Technology in Ongoing Professional Development

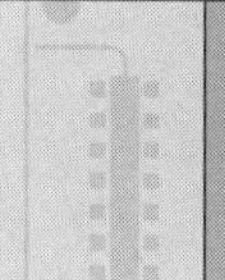

Performance Indicator V.A.

Use technology resources to engage in ongoing professional development and lifelong learning.

Why All the Fuss about Lifelong Learning?

At first glance, increasing requirements for ongoing professional development may seem like overkill. After all, "highly qualified teachers" as defined in No Child Left Behind must hold a bachelor's degree, and a full teaching credential or license, and prove competency in the content areas they teach. However, research clearly shows that teacher quality has a far greater impact on student performance than was previously understood. It may be no surprise that students in classes taught by effective teachers perform better academically than students in classes taught by less effective teachers. But did you know that students who are assigned to effective teachers over a period of several years make much greater gains than their past performance would predict?

Effective teachers have strong subject area knowledge, possess a deep understanding of pedagogy, come to class well prepared, keep students engaged, regularly monitor student progress, and have good classroom management skills. One reason these teachers are able to stay on top of their game is that they recognize the importance of lifelong learning. They realize they cannot effectively prepare students to be successful members of society if they aren't keeping up with changes and trends themselves.

Some experts estimate that to meet growing demands for school reform, you must devote 20% of your work time to professional study and collaboration. Using the traditional paradigm of professional development through special events, this expectation is impossible to meet. However, you can also sharpen your skills and improve practice by engaging in such activities as collaborative planning and reflection, observing in other classrooms and talking about what you see, and reading and discussing professional literature. Readily available technologies can be used to facilitate all these activities.

Formal Professional Development Activities

There's a place for formal professional development workshops, seminars, conferences, and classes that are scheduled outside the regular school day. This kind of activity encourages you to look beyond the boundaries of your own classrooms to survey emerging trends in education, hear new ideas, and develop professional networks. But funds and time are limited, so a growing number of teachers are turning to technology-based professional development solutions, including online courses, videoconferences, and Webinars.

Online Courses

Online courses often offer the option of college or continuing education credit, making them an attractive option for those of you who are renewing your credentials or want to earn credit for salary increases. Formal online courses have official starting and ending dates, but most are designed to allow participants to work at their own pace and convenience. Class enrollment is not limited to geographic regions, so you often have opportunities to "meet" colleagues from far-flung places. This enables hearing new points of view and learning new strategies for tackling important issues.

It's important to note, however, that the online learning environment is different from what most of you are accustomed to. The workload is usually heavier than in a traditional class, where attendance and participation in discussions are given some weight. The lack of face-to-face meetings makes it easier to put off assignments. Virtual discussions take more time than quick verbal exchanges.

To be a successful online learner, you must have strong basic technology skills, access to a fairly new computer, and the determination to make and stick to an independent work schedule. A high-speed Internet connection is not absolutely mandatory, but online course participants with slower connections often report frustrating delays in accessing course Web sites and downloading or uploading files.

Before investing in an online course of training, you may want to try one or more free courses to experience the flavor of online learning. Reputable sites such as Edutopia (www.edutopia.org), thirteen ed online (www.thirteen.org/edonline/), and Teacher-to-Teacher Digital Workshops (www.paec.org/teacher2teacher/) are good sources for free professional development modules.

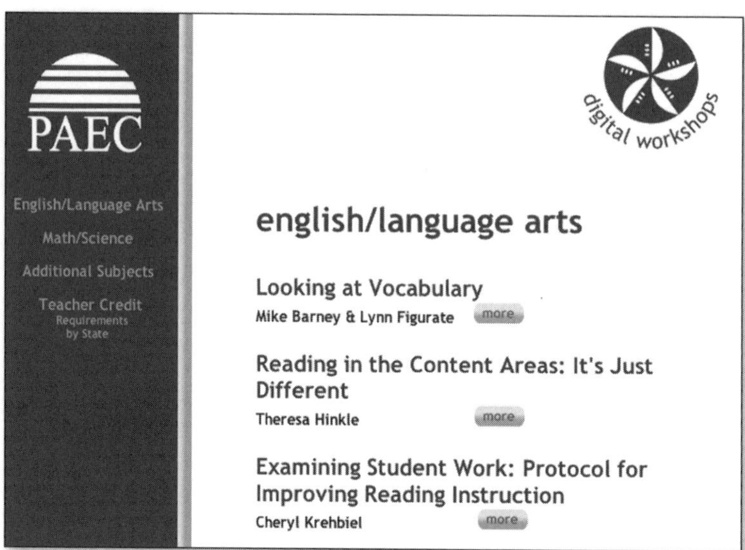

FIGURE 5.1 Free online workshops, conducted by nationally known educators, are available on the Teacher-to-Teacher Web site.

WEBINARS

Webinars are similar to 1-hour seminars or conference sessions, but they're delivered via the Internet. Live Webinars are designed to permit interaction between the presenter and the audience. Participation requires access to an Internet-connected computer. Regularly hosted by commercial vendors or educational organizations, Webinars are often free.

Following the initial presentation, these sessions may be archived, making it possible to view them at any time. For example, visit the TechLEARNING site at www.techlearning.com/events/ to access the Webinars archived there. Some professional conferences also archive selected sessions online. The National Educational Computing Conference (NECC) makes conference sessions available online for approximately 3 months following each year's conference.

VIDEOCONFERENCES

Videoconferencing involves the transmission of visuals and sound to two or more separate locations through the use of cameras, monitors, speakers, and microphones. Educational use of videoconferencing isn't a new idea, but many educators have little or no experience with it because special equipment is required to participate. In formal settings, usually sponsored by institutions of higher learning or regional and state offices of education, videoconferences are used to enable groups that meet in more than one location to participate in a shared learning experience, such as a class session or a virtual meeting. Videoconferences may also be archived for later viewing. Keep an eye on developments in this technology. Internet-based videoconferencing is bringing this technology down to the individual workstation level, dramatically lowering costs and increasing access.

PODCASTS

Another technology to consider is the podcast, which first became popular in 2004. Usually free, podcasts are audio files posted to the Web for users to download and listen to on a computer or MP3 player. Increasing numbers of educators are creating podcasts for a variety of purposes. You can find education-related podcasts at sites such as The Education Podcast Network (http://epnWeb.org) or Podcast Alley (www.podcastalley.com/podcast_genres.php).

Work-Embedded Professional Development Activities

In addition to formal professional development activities, you need to change your thinking about how daily activities can contribute to your overall professional growth. Collaborative planning time, classroom observations, and easy access to current professional literature are all strategies that can be built into the regular workday and facilitated through the use of technology to strengthen teaching skills.

COLLABORATIVE PLANNING

Most teachers welcome opportunities to meet with colleagues to discuss curriculum and engage in joint planning, but effective collaborative planning takes time. Use of an online tool called a wiki makes it possible for you to shorten face-to-face meeting time because it's possible to work on collaborative projects at times convenient for each individual.

Wikis are described more fully in this chapter under Performance Indicator V.C., but briefly, a wiki is a Web page where text can be added and edited by anyone who has access. This capability makes wikis an excellent tool for collaborative writing of lesson plans and other documents. Tim Fredrick's ELA Teaching Wiki (http://timfredrick.pbwiki.com) and Huff Lessons (http://hufflessons.pbwiki.com) are examples of wiki-based lesson plan collections. Both are pbwikis (http://pbwiki.com), password-protected sites that limit editing capabilities to users who have been given the password.

Here's an example of how a wiki can be used for online collaborative planning: Teachers in a grade level or departmental group agree to develop and share lesson plans for several instructional units. The group meets to select the units and set parameters for plan formats, timelines, and so forth. During the meeting, a volunteer uses a wiki page to record notes and set up a linked page for each teacher. These pages include a template for the unit and lesson plans. Each teacher uses an assigned wiki page to write plans, and supporting documentation (e.g., student activity pages) is uploaded and linked to the lessons as needed.

The pages are reviewed by all members of the group, who add suggestions or make edits on each page. Once the plans are drafted, the group meets again for a face-to-face discussion and final editing. Now the group has an online archive of unit lessons that can be accessed and used at any time. In the future, revisions can be made without having to start from scratch.

PEER OBSERVATIONS

Observing other teachers working in their classrooms is a valuable experience for any educator. Unfortunately, it's not always easy to release teachers to do peer observations. When I was an elementary principal, a group of my teachers met monthly to discuss implementation of several new language arts instructional strategies. They felt it would be beneficial to observe one another teaching lessons using the strategies and then discuss what they saw. It didn't take long before the logistics of scheduling and conducting multiple peer observations every month became a barrier.

The group proposed the following tech-based solution for this challenge: The school had three video cameras and tripods. The teachers agreed to tape themselves teaching lessons using the new strategies. These tapes were viewed and discussed during meetings. An unanticipated bonus was that a library of video examples gradually accumulated, and teachers could return to them when evaluating the success of the program.

ACCESS TO PROFESSIONAL LITERATURE

Every school needs to have a professional library where you can find up-to-date information about research, instructional strategies, sample lesson plans, and other topics. However, space and cost are often limiting factors. Online journals and other e-publications can provide greater access to professional literature than you might have otherwise.

For example, every major educational association now has a Web site where you can find recent articles and other important information. Most professional journals and magazines—*Technology & Learning* (www.techlearning.com) or *Learning & Leading with Technology* (www.iste.org), for example—offer similar online services. There are sites where video and audio clips are available as well, such as Edutopia (www.edutopia.org/magazine/). Many limit full access to members or subscribers, but most offer all visitors access to at least some resources.

One drawback to using online resources for professional reading is the time it takes to find them. A technology-based solution is to create an online bibliography or catalog of recommended articles, including links to the material. Free, Web-based bookmarking sites, such as backflip.com or del.icio.us.com, make it possible to save and share good links with just a few clicks of the mouse (see the Web-Based Bookmarking Services sidebar in chapter 2). The library/media specialist, leadership team, or volunteers can get the ball rolling by finding and bookmarking a few sites and then sharing the bibliography link with the staff. Teachers can be invited to add their favorite sites to the bibliography. In addition to facilitating link sharing, Web-based bookmarks can be accessed from any Internet-connected computer—anywhere, anytime. Using this kind of tool, a school's professional library can grow and be updated quickly.

These are just a few ways that you can use technology to engage in ongoing professional development and lifelong learning. New technologies to facilitate online learning and collaboration are announced regularly, so it's important to keep current with new trends. However, if you're using online resources regularly, you'll find that it's much easier to stay on top of new developments. Use the statements and questions in the following table to consider steps you might take to increase your use of technology to support formal and work-embedded professional development.

TABLE 5.1 ■ Performance Indicator V.A.

Use technology resources to engage in ongoing professional development and lifelong learning.

Directions: Rate each numbered statement or question using the scale provided, and give a Yes or No answer to question 4. Use the short-answer areas to respond to prompts.

Rating Scale (Statements 1 and 2): **1** = Never **2** = Seldom **3** = Sometimes **4** = Often **5** = Regularly (as appropriate)					
1. Technology resources are used to support formal professional development activities.	1	2	3	4	5
Describe how technology resources are used to support formal professional development activities:					
List the steps you will take to increase or improve the use of technology resources to support formal professional development activities:					
2. Technology resources are used to support work-embedded professional development activities.	1	2	3	4	5
Describe how technology resources are used to support work-embedded professional development activities.					

(Continued)

TABLE 5.1 ■ **Performance Indicator V.A.** *(Continued)*

<table>
<tr><td colspan="5">List the steps you will take to increase or improve the use of technology resources to support work-embedded professional development activities:</td></tr>
<tr><td colspan="5">Rating Scale (Question 3):
1 = No 2 = Yes, with help 3 = Yes 4 = Yes, and I could help others be successful</td></tr>
<tr><td rowspan="2">3. Would your current technology skills allow you to participate successfully in technology-supported professional development activities?</td><td>1</td><td>2</td><td>3</td><td>4</td></tr>
<tr><td></td><td></td><td></td><td></td></tr>
<tr><td rowspan="2">4. Have you successfully participated in technology-supported professional development activities?</td><td colspan="2">Yes</td><td colspan="2">No</td></tr>
<tr><td colspan="2"></td><td colspan="2"></td></tr>
<tr><td colspan="5">Describe your previous experience with technology-supported professional development activities:</td></tr>
<tr><td colspan="5">List the steps you will take to increase your current technology skills or increase or improve your participation in technology-supported professional development activities:</td></tr>
</table>

Reflecting on the Effectiveness of Technology Use in the Classroom

Performance Indicator V.B.

Continually evaluate and reflect on professional practice to make informed decisions regarding the use of technology in support of student learning.

Why Reflect?

Most teachers reflect on what they *plan* to teach. Many teachers reflect on what's happening *while* they're teaching. But truly effective teachers also take the time to reflect *after* the instructional day, when they can evaluate what transpired in the classroom and assess the impact on student performance. On your own, you can think about your experiences: what worked and what didn't work. You can also draw on your content knowledge and understanding of pedagogy to avoid focusing on technique at the expense of understanding the underlying values and assumptions that lead to daily practice.

But effective teachers don't work in isolation. A critical piece of reflective practice is taking the time to interact with colleagues, inviting opportunities to learn from their experiences and perhaps learn new approaches to problem solving. In the mid 1990s, experts began urging teachers to expand reflection through participation in Reflective Practice Groups (RPGs), as described by Schaak Distad, Chase, Germundsen, and Cady Brownstein (2000) (see the What is a Reflective Practice Group? sidebar in chapter 4).

How Does this Relate to Technology Use?

Despite the fact that desktop computers began appearing in classrooms nearly 4 decades ago, effective use of instructional technology is still a major challenge for many teachers. Leaving folks to figure things out on their own hasn't worked well. Research shows that for technology use to enhance student performance, activities need to be more than automations of traditional tasks.

This means that you must be willing to make significant changes in how you organize and run your classrooms. Unfortunately, many of you haven't had access to good, replicable models for appropriate instructional technology use. As a result, you've tended to fall back on instructional strategies used by *your* teachers, few or none of whom were implementing technology in meaningful ways.

Add to this the accelerating rate of change in this field, and it's highly unlikely that even the most motivated educators among you will be able to keep up with all the new trends in educational technology on your own. Participation in a formal or informal RPG can go a long way toward helping you learn how to use technology to support student learning and to evaluate that use. Questions to address on a regular basis in an RPG setting include:

1. How am I incorporating the use of technology as an instructional and learning tool?
2. What research base supports the teaching strategies I'm using?
3. Why did I decide to use instructional technology in this way?
4. Does this strategy have a positive impact on students' understanding of the content?
5. If yes, how do I know that? If no, how do I know that, and what do I need to change?

Embedding the RPG into Regular Practice

You may be saying to yourself, "Great! Another meeting. I'm sure my colleagues will be eager to add something else to their jammed schedules." But group reflection is a *process*, not a separate activity. By restructuring the format for grade-level, departmental, and full faculty meetings, it's possible to engage in group reflection without adding another meeting.

For example, the Performance Indicator V.A. discussion earlier in this chapter includes a description of a group of elementary teachers who met monthly to discuss new teaching strategies. Although it wasn't called an RPG, that's exactly what it was. The teachers who attended those meetings represented five grade levels (K–4), and the site administrator was included. Members' teaching experience ranged from 2 years to more than 20 years.

The purpose of the meetings was to monitor implementation of new instructional strategies, including the use of various technologies to support teaching and assessment, and to evaluate their impact on student achievement. The work accomplished in this context strengthened the teachers' skills and resulted in increased student performance in an environment where technology was one of several tools used by teachers and students.

Individual teachers don't control how general faculty meetings are conducted, but the documented success of RPGs makes it worth bringing the idea to site administrators. Even if general faculty meetings aren't restructured, you do influence how departmental or grade-level meetings are planned, and you have little patience for meetings that are largely a waste of time. Using the RPG process is a way to bring value to regular meetings and explore technology integration in a meaningful context.

Use the statements in the following table to consider steps you might take to continually evaluate and reflect on professional practice to make informed decisions regarding the use of technology in support of student learning.

TABLE 5.2 ■ Performance Indicator V.B.

Continually evaluate and reflect on professional practice to make informed decisions regarding the use of technology in support of student learning.

Directions: Rate each numbered statement using the scale provided. Use the short-answer areas to respond to prompts.

Rating Scale: 1 = Never 2 = Seldom 3 = Sometimes 4 = Often 5 = Daily					
1. I reflect on the decisions I make regarding the use of technology in support of student learning while I am planning lessons.	1	2	3	4	5
Describe how you decide when to use technology in support of student learning:					
List the steps you will take to increase or improve the reflection you do during lesson planning:					
2. I reflect on how technology use is working to support student learning during a lesson.	1	2	3	4	5
Describe how you gauge the impact of technology use during a lesson:					

(Continued)

TABLE 5.2 ■ **Performance Indicator V.B.** *(Continued)*

	1	2	3	4	5
List the steps you will take to increase or improve the reflection you do during lesson implementation:					
3. I evaluate and reflect on the decisions I've made regarding the use of technology in support of student learning after the lesson is taught.					
Describe how you evaluate and reflect upon the decisions you've made regarding the use of technology in support of student learning after the lesson is taught:					
List the steps you will take to increase or improve the reflection you do after a lesson is taught:					

Increasing Productivity with Technology

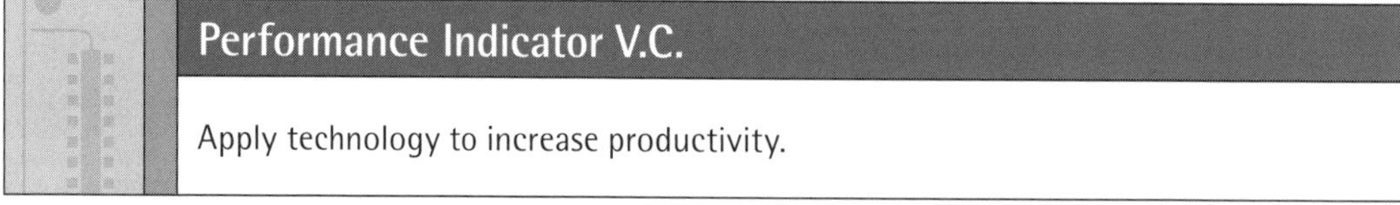

Performance Indicator V.C.
Apply technology to increase productivity.

You are increasingly using technology tools to improve your personal productivity, according to a survey conducted by CDW Government, Inc. (2005). Administrative uses of technology included sending e-mails to parents, taking attendance, and posting grades and general information about classes online. You also reported that the majority of effective technology-related professional development you received focused on how to use e-mail and word processing. Interestingly, at least in this study, most of the training and use seems to focus on the automation of traditional tasks rather than on using technology to deal with information in new ways.

Increased productivity needs to mean more than doing the same things faster. Not only can you work more effectively when you use tools that change the way you approach a task, but you're also in a better position to understand why similar changes in instructional strategies will have greater impact on students' engagement and performance. Here are a few low- or no-cost Web-based tools you can use to increase not just the quantity of work done, but also its quality. The Web-based tools list in the resources section found at the end of this chapter provides links to several specific examples.

Weblogs, or Blogs

Free or low-cost blogs can be used for private writing by one author. Or, they can be used to establish an online community where readers are invited to comment on posted writings or author-original posts themselves (see the Definitions sidebar in chapter 3). A single-author private blog is a good venue for individual reflective practice. Group blogs, with single or multiple authors, are designed to share information and gather input. These work well as a replacement for staff bulletins, or as an alternative to more traditional classroom Web sites.

You don't need to be a programmer to set up and maintain a blog. Adding new posts, or commenting on existing posts, requires only the time needed to type the text and click a button. Depending on the blog tool used, it's possible to categorize and search entries, moderate comments, limit access to an invited group (e.g., fellow staff members or parents), notify invited members electronically when a new post or comment has been added, and more.

Wikis

Wikis are very useful for collaborative writing projects, such as plan updates or grant proposals (see the Definitions sidebar in chapter 3). While wikis were originally completely open to the public, online hosts can now offer private, password-secured wikis. Although any password holder can make changes, edits are tracked, and earlier versions of a document can be restored. A few wiki sites offer page-locking. In this case, the original author locks a page to deny editing privileges to all other users.

Setting up a wiki doesn't require programming skills. A few simple editing conventions will be explained on the site's Help or Frequently Asked Questions (FAQs) area. Large writing projects such as grant proposals can be broken into smaller sections that are linked together by creating a table of contents. Most wiki hosts offer a title-search feature, and some include full text-searching capabilities.

Online Collaborative Groups

Online collaborative groups enable users to engage in a variety of different activities. Features vary from one host site to another, but they commonly include a shared calendar, to-do lists, e-mail capabilities, a place for notes or messages, and file posting. Some also allow users to send reminder messages to their cell phones. These sites are useful for project planning, communication between meetings, sharing Web links, and other work-related tasks.

Online groups are easy to set up using online templates. The group organizer invites members to join via e-mail. Options often allow the organizer to keep the group private, moderate or edit postings, or assign levels of access to different members. Some free hosts (e.g., Yahoo! and Groups) post ads on group sites, but others (e.g., AirSet) are ad-free. This would be especially important to consider if you decide to set up a group for communication between home and school.

Voice over Internet Protocol

Classrooms don't always come equipped with a telephone, and even when they do, district systems often block long-distance calls. This is problematic when you need to contact parents or colleagues outside the local calling area. Skype is a free Voice over Internet Protocol (VoIP) system that enables users to make voice calls using a computer. You need an Internet-connected computer, a headset with a microphone, and a sound card.

Computer-to-computer calls are free. Computer to landline or cell phones cost roughly 2 cents per minute. Add a free plug-in called Festoon, and a Web cam, and you can make video calls. The possibilities for professional collaboration and instruction using these tools are wide open.

Other promising technologies for enhancing productivity in meaningful ways include mobile devices. For example, you can use a handheld computer to easily gather assessment data and then beam the information to another computer or a printer. Using a spreadsheet or similar program, you can focus on data analysis rather than on the mechanics of data collection and entry. Tablet computers, which allow users to use a special stylus to write directly on the monitor screen, increase your mobility and can significantly reduce the time required to collect and enter data. This handwriting recognition capability is especially useful for science, math, and language teachers, who frequently use special symbols. Other features of special software for tablets enable users to manipulate documents in ways not possible with traditional desktop and laptop computers.

It would be impossible to describe all the ways you can use technology to enhance professional practice. The really important point in this discussion is the fact that you need to think beyond automation. This focus on doing the same old thing a bit more efficiently is a major cause of the disconnect between teacher use of technology and student use of technology. While some may never truly believe that tiny PDA (personal digital assistant) screens are suitable for sustained reading and writing, by expanding your use of technology you can get a glimpse of what students take for granted: technology redefines the way we do business.

Use the statements and questions in the following table to consider steps you might take to apply technology to increase productivity.

TABLE 5.3 ■ **Performance Indicator V.C.**
Apply technology to increase productivity.

Directions: Use your responses to these statements and questions to reflect on your use of technology to increase productivity and to identify steps you might take to increase or enhance this usage.

1. List the three technologies you use most frequently to increase personal productivity:
2. List the three technologies used to increase personal productivity that you value most:
3. How do these technologies increase your personal productivity? Are you automating a traditional task, or using information in a new way? Explain:
4. How could you expand use of these technologies to use information in a different way?
5. List three steps you will take to either learn a new technology or enhance your use of a technology you now use:

Communicating and Collaborating Using Technology

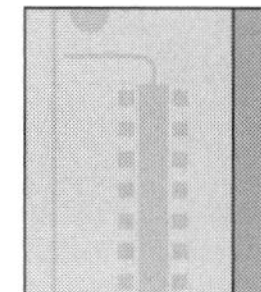

Performance Indicator V.D.

Use technology to communicate and collaborate with peers, parents, and the larger community in order to nurture student learning.

In the last 10 years, Internet use has exploded. Here are a few recent statistics:

- 68% of American adults use the Internet
- 87% of American teens use the Internet
- 99% of U.S. schools now have Internet access
- 98% of teachers report that their districts provide them with e-mail accounts
- 53% of all Internet users report having high-speed access
- 91% of Internet users send and receive e-mail
- an estimated 42 billion e-mails are sent daily (in contrast, the U.S. Postal Service handled approximately 670 million pieces of mail in 2002)
- 84% of all Internet users use search engines to find Web sites
- the number of Web sites has grown to more than 60 million from 37 million in the last 3 years
- 27% of all Internet users read Weblogs, or blogs

Web-based tools, such as e-mail, blogs, Listservs, discussion groups, and forums, have made communication possible at levels that were once unimaginable. With very little effort you can

- seek advice from experts in nearly any field,
- share ideas with other educators anywhere in the world,
- post notices for parents, and
- spotlight student work for the community.

However, it's still rare to find a school where, to support student learning, all staff members make regular, effective use of electronic communication to collaborate with peers, parents, and the larger community.

Regardless of the reasons educators may have given in the past for avoiding professional use of electronic communication, things have changed. The resources are out there. The majority of families have access to the Internet. It's time to get started.

Collaborating with Peers

Several tools for peer collaboration via electronic communication were discussed earlier in this chapter, including blogs, wikis, online work groups, and VoIP. However, that discussion focused primarily on communication with groups, either at one site or within one district.

These tools can also be used to foster communication outside the district. You may not feel comfortable starting up your own blog or wiki to begin collaboration, but that's not necessary. Numerous online resources invite teachers to lurk (read postings) or join in on existing discussions. Here are a few examples:

> Ed-Tech Insider (www.eschoolnews.com/eti/): This multi-authored blog hosted by eSchool News covers a variety of education topics.
>
> Webblogg-ed (www.Weblogg-ed.com): Educator Will Richardson shares his thoughts about education and technology.
>
> Bud Hunt's Wiki (http://budtheteacher.com/wiki/): Teacher Bud Hunt and other contributors are using this wiki to create classroom resources.
>
> Teacher Mailring Center (http://teachers.net/mailrings/): Sponsored by Teachers.net, educators may subscribe to a variety of e-mail Listservs to engage in discussions with other teachers around the world.
>
> Teachnology Teacher Forums (www.teach-nology.com/forum/): These forums offer educators free online discussions covering Grades K–12, as well as special groups for new or student teachers and classroom pen pal exchanges.

Collaborating with Parents and the Larger Community

All teachers need to explore strategies for making information available to parents and students via the Internet. If you're just getting started with electronic communication, you may want to start with a simple e-mail list. Most e-mail programs offer the option of creating mailing lists. Collect parent e-mail addresses, set up a group, and start distributing newsletters or other regular communiqués using your e-mail list.

A simple blog can also be used to share this kind of information. Check with your tech support staff to get their recommendations for blogging software and setup. Most blogs can be set up in less than 15 minutes, and you can begin posting right away. Share the URL with parents, and you're all set. Whether you use an e-mail list or a blog, be sure to set realistic objectives for yourself. It's better to promise monthly contact, but do more, than to guarantee weekly messages and fall behind.

Classroom Web sites are popular with parents and students. These sites are also a good way to share information with the community at large. However, a Web site can be a lot of work. Many teachers are using blogs rather than traditional Web sites because they're easier to set up and maintain. Again, talk with tech support staff to find out what's possible in your district. Think about the kinds of information you want or need to share with parents and students. You might even survey these groups to identify the items they would look for on a classroom site. Start small and add new areas as you determine what's needed and the amount of time it will take to add and maintain new content. Here are a few examples:

> Carmack's Critters (www.butlerville.net/1a/): First-grade blog.
>
> Elizabeth Fullerton.com (www.elizabethfullerton.com): High school English class blog.
>
> Sixth-Grade Communication Arts with Miss Ryan (http://missryan.matt-morris.com): Sixth-grade Web site.

Before initiating or expanding your use of online communication tools, check your district's Acceptable Use Policy (AUP) and talk with your administrator about your plans. Ask about district policies related to archiving e-mail, posting student work or photos online, and any other restrictions you can think of. Refer to Performance Indicator VI.A. in chapter 6 for additional information about policies for online use. Be sure to secure administrator approval, and then proceed.

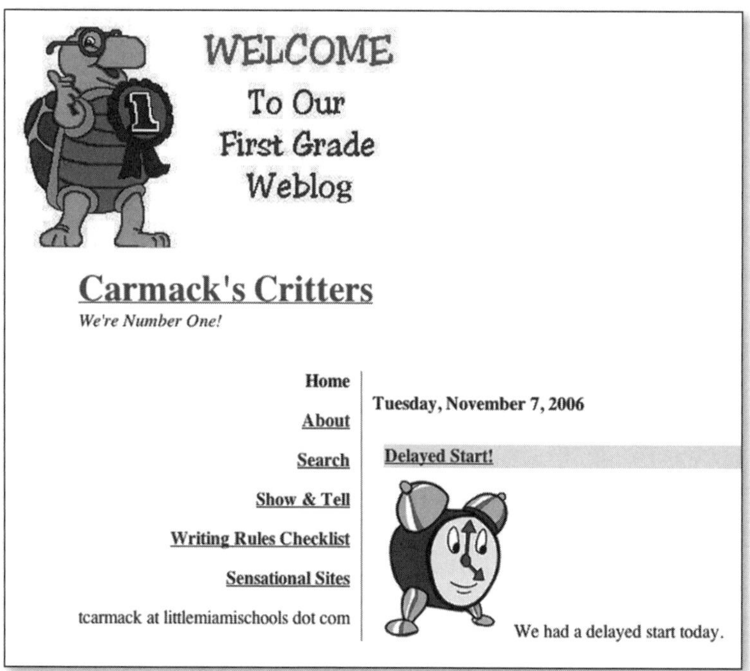

FIGURE 5.2 Ms. Carmack, first-grade teacher at Butlerville Elementary School in Blanchester, Ohio, keeps parents updated on classroom activities using her blog.

Use the statements in the following table to consider steps you might take to use technology to communicate and collaborate with peers, parents, and the larger community to nurture student learning.

TABLE 5.4 ■ Performance Indicator V.D.

Use technology to communicate and collaborate with peers, parents, and the larger community in order to nurture student learning.

Directions: Rate each numbered statement using the scale provided. Use the short-answer areas to respond to prompts.

Rating Scale: **1** = Never **2** = Seldom **3** = Sometimes **4** = Often **5** = Regularly (as appropriate)					
1. I use technology to communicate and collaborate with peers.	1	2	3	4	5
Describe your use of technology to communicate and collaborate with peers:					
List the steps you will take to initiate or enhance the use of technology to communicate and collaborate with peers:					
2. I use technology to communicate and collaborate with parents and the larger community.	1	2	3	4	5
Describe your use of technology to communicate and collaborate with parents and the larger community:					
List the steps you will take to initiate or enhance the use of technology to communicate and collaborate with parents and the larger community:					

Action Plan

Now that you've read about each performance indicator for Standard V and have had the opportunity to think about your level of implementation for each indicator, it's time to develop an action plan to improve or expand your professional practice in each area.

Review your responses to the statements and questions in each performance indicator table. It's not possible to master every indicator at once, so choose one at a time. Build your plan using the steps you identified you might take for the chosen performance indicator and complete your action plan by using the table below. Performance Indicator V.D. has been used as a sample.

TABLE 5.5 ■ **Teachers use technology to enhance their productivity and professional practice**

Performance Indicator	Next Steps	I need to work on this step with the following people...	I will know this step has been achieved when...	Timeline
V.D. Use technology to communicate and collaborate with peers, parents, and the larger community in order to nurture student learning.	*Review and subscribe to several education blogs to connect with other teachers.*	*Other department members and the district technology specialist, to get names of blogs they recommend.*	*I have found and subscribed to at least three blogs and have posted at least one comment on each blog I subscribe to.*	*2 weeks.*
	1.			
	2.			
	3.			

Resources

ARTICLES AND REPORTS

Bailey, Kathleen M. (1997). Reflective teaching: Situating our stories. [Online article]. *Asian Journal of English Language Teaching*, Vol. 7. Available: www.cuhk.edu.hk/ajelt/vol7/art1.htm.

CDW Government, Inc. (2005). *Teachers Talk Technology 2005.* [Online report]. Available: http://newsroom.cdwg.com/features/feature-08-29-05.htm

Education Week.(2005). *Electronic transfer: Moving technology dollars in new directions.* [Online report]. Available: www.edweek.org/ew/toc/2005/05/05/index.html.

Levin, Douglas, and Sousan, Arafeh. (2002, August 14). *The digital disconnect.* [Online report]. Available: www.pewInternet.org/pdfs/PIP_Schools_Internet_Report.pdf

NetDay. (2004, May 12). Insights and ideas of teachers on technology: NetDay national report on speak up day for teachers 2004. [Online report].
Available: www.netday.org/SPEAKUP/pdfs/NETDaySUD4T2004Report.pdf

Pew Internet & American Life Project. (2005). *Demographics of Internet users: May–June 2005 tracking survey.* [Online report].
Available: www.pewInternet.org/trends/User_Demo_08.09.05.htm

Pew Internet & American Life Project. (2005). *Internet activities: March 2000 to present tracking survey.* [Online report]. Available: www.pewInternet.org/trends/Internet_Activities_8.05.05.htm

Rothman, Robert. (2004, January/February). *Landing the "highly qualified teacher."* [Online article]. Harvard Education Letter. Available: www.edletter.org/past/issues/2004-jf/hiring.shtml

Schaak Distad, Linda; Chase, Betsy; Germundsen, Richard; and Cady Brownstein, Joan. (2000). Putting their heads together. [Online article]. *Journal of Staff Development*, Vol. 21, No. 4.
Available: www.nsdc.org/library/publications/jsd/distad214.cfm

Tice, Julie. (2005). *Reflective teaching: Exploring our own classroom practice.* [Online article]. Teaching English, BBC|British Council.
Available: www.teachingenglish.org.uk/think/methodology/reflection.shtml

Wenglinsky, Harold. (1998). *Does it compute? The relationship between educational technology and student achievement in mathematics.* [Online article]. Educational Testing Services.
Available: http://caret.iste.org/index.cfm?StudyID=337&fuseaction=studySummary/

BOOKS

Harris, Jim, and Brannick, Joan. (1999). *Finding and keeping great employees.* New York: AMA Publications.

WEB-BASED TOOLS

Backflip: www.backflip.com

Backpack: www.backpackit.com

Blogger.com (Google): www.blogger.com

Class Blogmeister: http://classblogmeister.com

Del.icio.us: http://del.icio.us/

Edublogs.org: http://edublogs.org

The Education Podcast Network: http://epnWeb.org

Festoon: www.festooninc.com

Pbwiki (PeanutButter wiki): http://pbwiki.com

Podcast Alley: www.podcastalley.com/podcast_genres.php

WEB SITES

National Education Association (NEA). *No Child Left Behind (ESEA): Teacher and paraprofessional quality.* Available: www.nea.org/esea/eseateach.html

North Central Regional Educational Laboratory. (1997). *Pathways critical issue: Finding time for professional development.*
Available: www.ncrel.org/sdrs/areas/issues/educatrs/profdevl/pd300.htm

U.S. Department of Education. (2005). *New No Child Left Behind flexibility: Highly qualified teachers.* Available: www.ed.gov/nclb/methods/teachers/hqtflexibility.html

U.S. Department of Labor: Bureau of Labor Statistics. (1998). *Occupational outlook handbook: Teachers—preschool, kindergarten, elementary, middle, and secondary.*
Available: http://stats.bls.gov/oco/ocos069.htm

Chapter 6

STANDARD VI

Social, Ethical, Legal, and Human Issues

Teachers understand the social, ethical, legal, and human issues surrounding the use of technology in PK–12 schools and apply those principles in practice.

PERFORMANCE INDICATORS FOR TEACHERS

VI.A. Model and teach legal and ethical practice related to technology use.

VI.B. Apply technology resources to enable and empower learners with diverse backgrounds, characteristics, and abilities.

VI.C. Identify and use technology resources that affirm diversity.

VI.D. Promote safe and healthy use of technology resources.

VI.E. Facilitate equitable access to technology resources for all students.

Chapter 6 Overview

Increased access to and use of technology at home and at school brings to light new issues and concerns for teachers and administrators. In those instances where a student hacks into your online grade book or attempts to upload unauthorized software onto a school computer, the consequences are relatively easy to determine and implement. But establishing the school's scope of authority related to inappropriate postings on students' blogs and Web sites isn't so clear.

Before cut and paste made it easy to copy large blocks of text, intentional plagiarism required a lot of work. Now an entire research paper can be cobbled together from multiple resources in a matter of minutes. As a result, some students don't understand the difference between research notes and copyright violations.

Cell phones, MP3 players, and handheld computers are a fact of life for students off campus. Inventive teachers are finding effective strategies for classroom use of these devices, but some students abuse these technologies to cheat on exams or engage in cyber-bullying.

These are just a few examples of the kinds of problems today's teachers must reckon with on a daily basis. In addition, there are questions about equal access to technology and access to materials that affirm diversity, as well as concerns about the relationship between technology use and repetitive stress injuries, such as carpal tunnel syndrome or gamer's thumb.

The performance indicators for this standard focus on your understanding of the social, ethical, legal, and human issues surrounding the use of technology in schools. Educators who model and teach legal and ethical practice; use technology to empower all students, regardless of background or ability; and promote safe, healthy use of technology prepare their students for a lifetime of appropriate technology use. Meeting these performance indicators requires you to reflect on your instructional practice and identify areas of strength, as well as areas where improvements can be made, in order to cope with the changes wrought by increased technology use.

Modeling Legal and Ethical Technology Use

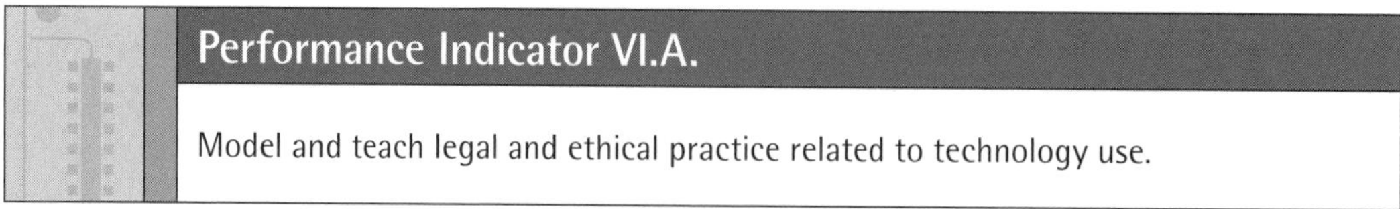

Performance Indicator VI.A.

Model and teach legal and ethical practice related to technology use.

Most schools today accept federal education funds or E-rate funding, or both. This means that they're required to have an Acceptable Use Policy (AUP) in place for staff and students. An AUP is a formal set of rules for using technologies provided by the district. AUPs spell out the consequences for violating these rules. The rules are usually quite specific and, at a minimum, cover use of the Internet, electronic communication (e.g., e-mail, instant messaging, chat), system hacking, and Internet safety. They may also include a copyright and plagiarism policy.

Adults and children are held to different standards when it comes to certain aspects of online use. For example, federal regulations allow districts to offer leveled filtering so that adults can access Web sites not available to students. Or, incidental personal use of school technology may be permitted for adults, but not students. Suitable disciplinary actions for adults may differ from appropriate disciplinary actions for students.

For these and other reasons, it makes sense for districts to have separate AUPs for staff and students. For the district's own protection, staff members should be expected to review and sign the AUP each school year. This provides a regular opportunity to ensure that the rules outlined in the AUP are appropriate and that staff members understand the policy. Pay special attention to any provisions that deal with blogs, Web sites, wikis, or other online postings that relate to school in any way.

To ensure that the policy can actually be enforced, student AUPs should be signed by both students and parents every year. Since most students are minors, it's wise for school sites to offer informational meetings for parents in conjunction with this annual signing. You also need to review the AUP with your students at least once every semester and remind them about the rules whenever the opportunity arises.

Students and adults often misunderstand the scope of the school's authority when it comes to personal blogs, Web sites, wikis, e-mail, and other online postings that relate to school in any way. For example, high school students who participate in extracurricular activities that prohibit any use of alcohol have faced disciplinary action at school for using their "private" blogs to post photos of drinking parties that occurred off-campus and on the weekend. Pay special attention to any provisions of the AUP that deal directly with these issues. In addition, be very clear about student use of mobile technologies such as cell phones, digital cameras, and MP3 players. Students have faced disciplinary action for simply having these items on campuses where possession of one of these devices is prohibited, whether or not it ever leaves a student's backpack.

Encouraging legal and ethical behavior requires more than a signature and a few lessons on acceptable use. You need to model this kind of behavior every time technology is used. Following copyright guidelines is an area where educators are often tempted to push the envelope. What if you have a license to run a software program on 30 computers but have 31 students who need to use the program simultaneously? Installing the program on that 31st system may be expedient, but it would also be illegal in this case. Want to liven up your classroom Web page with a few graphics? It's fine to use images from public domain collections, but if you post copyrighted pictures of a popular cartoon character and don't pay for the rights, you're violating the law.

Adults sometimes hedge on AUP rules as well. Does the district AUP forbid personal use of the Internet during the school day? If so, it's not okay to check an online auction or personal e-mail during lunchtime. We may think they're not paying attention, but students do notice this kind of behavior. Our actions always speak far louder than our words.

Most important, stay actively engaged with your students as they work online. Monitor their use by walking around the room, and check the browser history or cache after class to see where they've been. Teach them the difference between summarizing information and copying text verbatim, as well as how to properly cite online resources. A good resource for learning more about electronic copyright issues is Copyright with Cyberbee (www.cyberbee.com/copyrt.html).

Let students know that you care about their safety by teaching proper Netiquette (good online manners). Just as you have rules for classroom behavior, you need to establish rules for students' online behavior that include being polite during online discussions and in e-mail exchanges, respecting privacy by not posting personal information about themselves or others, proofreading posts and e-mails before they're submitted, asking for clarification when an online remark is unclear, and being supportive of members of the online community. You may want to review the following online resources for further information:

- Netiquette Home Page—www.albion.com/netiquette/
- Netiquette for Kids—www.bpl.org/kids/Netiquette.htm

Finally, be sure that you enforce your AUP consistently and fairly. Students will make mistakes. These can be opportunities to teach them legal and ethical use of technology before things get out of hand. But in order to do this, students need to know that you care and that you're holding them to the same standards you follow yourself. See this chapter's resources section for links to more information about copyright and Internet safety.

Use the following table to identify ways you model and teach legal and ethical practice related to technology use.

TABLE 6.1 ■ Performance Indicator VI.A.

Model and teach legal and ethical practice related to technology use.

Directions: Give a Yes or No answer to the numbered statements. Use the short-answer areas to elaborate on your answers.

Statement	Yes	No
1. My district or school has an Acceptable Use Policy (AUP) for staff members.		
2. Staff members are required to sign the AUP every year.		
3. I fully understand the provisions of the AUP for adults.		
Describe the steps you take to model compliance with the AUP:		
List the steps you will take to improve the way you model compliance with the AUP:		
4. My district or school has an AUP for students.		
5. Students and their parents are required to sign the AUP every year.		
6. I fully understand the provisions of the AUP for students.		
Describe the steps you take to teach students how to comply with the AUP:		

(Continued)

TABLE 6.1 ■ **Performance Indicator VI.A.** *(Continued)*

List the steps you will take to improve the way you teach students to comply with the AUP:		
7. My district or school has a Copyright and Plagiarism Policy.	**Yes**	**No**
8. I fully understand the provisions of the Copyright and Plagiarism Policy for staff and students.	**Yes**	**No**
Describe the steps you take to model compliance with the Copyright and Plagiarism Policy:		
List the steps you will take to improve the way you model compliance with the Copyright and Plagiarism Policy:		
Describe the steps you take to teach students to comply with the Copyright and Plagiarism Policy:		
List the steps you will take to improve the way you teach students to comply with the Copyright and Plagiarism Policy:		

Differentiating Instruction for All Learners with Technology

Performance Indicator VI.B.

Apply technology resources to enable and empower learners with diverse backgrounds, characteristics, and abilities.

Schools today serve an increasingly diverse student body. Technology can be used to level the playing field for students who face challenges related to language, cultural differences, learning style, and varying levels of ability. Whether selecting Web sites and software or developing your own technology-based instructional materials, here are four things you need to remember:

1. Using audio and visuals: Nearly all students engage with instructional materials that incorporate good use of sound and graphics. Look for these features in Web sites and software, but don't overlook the fact that it's also easy to add these features using programs such as Microsoft Office. Adding graphics to files created with these applications is as easy as cut and paste, and it's not difficult to incorporate sound, either. For example, PowerPoint users can add sound effects and narration to slides using the features of Insert Movies and Insert Sounds. It's also possible to add narration to a Word document by inserting a voice comment. In Excel, users can set a Text to Speech command that will read the content of cells aloud. A microphone, sound card, and speakers are required to take advantage of these features.

2. Writing to learn: Students can organize their thinking and express themselves more clearly when they've had time to write or draw their ideas. Graphic organizers, e-mail, blog entries, and word processing are just a few of the tools that can help students get their thoughts in writing and share them with fellow classmates. Older students who are learning a second language have commented that it's often easier for them to track and understand online discussions than take part in face-to-face discussions where they're trying to interpret what's being said and formulate a response at the same time.

3. Learning by doing: Students of any age learn more when they do something as opposed to just listening to a lecture. It's easy to find or develop hands-on, technology-based activities to help students increase their skills in technology and their content knowledge. For example, you can search online lesson libraries such as AT&T's Knowledge Network Explorer's Blue Web'N (www.filamentality.com/wired/bluewebn/) or WebQuest News (http://Webquest.org) to find existing content-based, technology-supported activities that address content. Or, you can create your own Web-based activities using tools such as Filamentality (www.filamentality.com/wired/fil/) and TrackStar (http://trackstar.4teachers.org/trackstar/). Be sure materials selected require student interaction.

4. Learning cooperatively: When students enter the workforce, they're going to be expected to function in environments where teamwork is the norm. It's important to afford students opportunities to work in small groups through their K–12 experience. Furthermore, research shows that when students use technology in this kind of environment, the technology use has a positive impact on student learning. Does this mean that every project must be completely technology-based? No. It means that students need to have access to a variety of technologies and know which to use and when.

The Individuals with Disabilities Education Act (IDEA) requires schools to provide additional support to students with severe learning or physical disabilities. Assistive technologies are designed to make curriculum materials and activities accessible to these students. These products include software and hardware that enable students to function more independently and successfully in the classroom. You have literally thousands of assistive technologies to choose from, including items such as alternative keyboards, special data entry devices, and software specially designed for use by students with impaired vision or hearing. If you have one or more students in your class who receive special services, you need to read their Individual Education Plans (IEPs) to see if the use of assistive technology has been included. It would also be helpful do some research on your own to identify resources you might use to provide additional instructional support (see the resources section at the end of the chapter).

Use the following table to identify ways you apply technology resources to enable and empower learners with diverse backgrounds, characteristics, and abilities.

TABLE 6.2 ■ **Performance Indicator VI.B.**

Apply technology resources to enable and empower learners with diverse backgrounds, characteristics, and abilities.

Directions: Give a Yes or No answer to question 4, and use the short-answer areas to respond to each prompt or question.

	Yes	No
1. List the technology resources you use to enable and empower learners with diverse backgrounds, characteristics, and abilities:		
2. Which of the resources you've listed are most effective? Explain:		
3. Which of the resources you've listed are least effective? Explain:		
4. Have you ever used assistive technology with students?		
Explain:		

Affirming Diversity with Technology

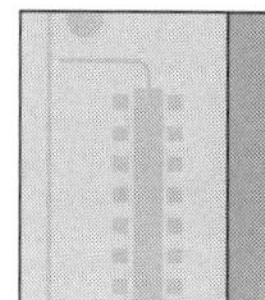

Performance Indicator VI.C.

Identify and use technology resources that affirm diversity.

The civil rights movement of the 1960s brought to all educators' attention the importance of acknowledging the fact that our students represent a wide range of social, racial, and cultural backgrounds. Since then, we've also become much more sensitive to issues of gender equity and students with special needs, both physical and intellectual. Educators need to demonstrate understanding of these differences by using materials and activities that affirm diversity. An excellent resource for keeping up-to-date on current research related to equity and diversity issues is Baltimore County Public Schools' Office of Equity and Assurance (www.bcps.org/offices/oea/publications/). This office regularly posts links to downloadable publications.

Progress has been made in this area, but there are still students who believe they encounter subtle, and not-so-subtle, forms of bias at school. There's no one best solution to the challenge of dealing with these differences, and more is required than simply choosing the "right" materials. However, teachers who make a practice of keeping these issues in mind and incorporating materials and practices that demonstrate sensitivity are on the right path. Due to limited space in this book, the following discussion is restricted to identifying and using technology resources that affirm diversity.

Here are some questions to ask when selecting software, Web sites, and other resources.

- Is the language used in the resource gender-neutral and free of stereotypes?
- Does the material include perspectives or contributions of people from various socioeconomic and ethnic groups?
- Are the cultural and literary references included in the material understandable to students of diverse backgrounds?
- Is the material accessible to students who are English Language Learners and those who have reading or physical disabilities?

If the answer to any of these questions is no, you need to consider whether it's possible to present the material in a context that acknowledges or explains the negatives. For example, you want students to read several primary source documents for a social studies lesson on the Wounded Knee Massacre. You find an online source for an editorial about the death of Sitting Bull, written by L. Frank Baum and published in 1890. While the text reflects stereotypes of that era and draws conclusions that are unacceptable today, it can be used to launch a discussion about prejudices that existed at the time. To use this primary source effectively, take the time to point out the publication date and discuss the prevailing social views of the time.

Also, the language is somewhat antiquated and may pose a problem for some students. Use a text-to-speech reader to make the material more accessible to these students. Since the document is in the public domain, you might copy and paste the text into a word processing document and ask students to highlight references they don't understand. You can also increase font size for students who have difficulty reading smaller type.

In cases where the issues can't be resolved, look for something else. With hundreds of programs and millions of Web sites, it's possible to find relevant materials that affirm diversity.

Use the following table to identify ways you identify and use technology resources that affirm diversity.

TABLE 6.3 ■ **Performance Indicator VI.C.**
Identify and use technology resources that affirm diversity.

Directions: Use the short-answer areas to respond to each statement or question.

1. List the strategies you employ to identify and use technology resources that affirm diversity:
2. Which of the strategies you've listed are most effective? Explain:
3. Which of the strategies you've listed are least effective? Explain:
4. Describe methods you use to present material within a context that acknowledges, explains, or rectifies diversity issues:

Promoting Safe and Healthy Technology Use

Performance Indicator VI.D.

Promote safe and healthy use of technology resources.

Until very recently, little thought was given to the physical impact of technology use on students and their teachers. Most students and teachers don't use computers long enough during the school day to cause themselves physical harm, but with increased access at home, the possibility of computer-related injuries is on the rise. Appropriate use of technology at school can help both students and teachers become more aware of their work environments at home.

What do you need to consider? Furniture, lighting, and type of hardware are all things that need some thought. Is your desk or table the right height? What about your chair? Do you have ample lighting that doesn't produce glare on the monitor screen? What kinds of computers are you using (desktop, laptop, handheld), and what adjustments in positioning can be made when using them? The Starfield Group, Inc., offers a free online ergonomics adjustment program for K–12 schools at www.ergostar.com/K–12.shtml. All teachers and students Grades 5 and up can access this program to learn more about ergonomically correct computer workstations. Another resource is the Oregon Occupational Safety and Health Division's *Computer Ergonomics for Elementary School*, accessible at www.orosha.org/cergos/index.html.

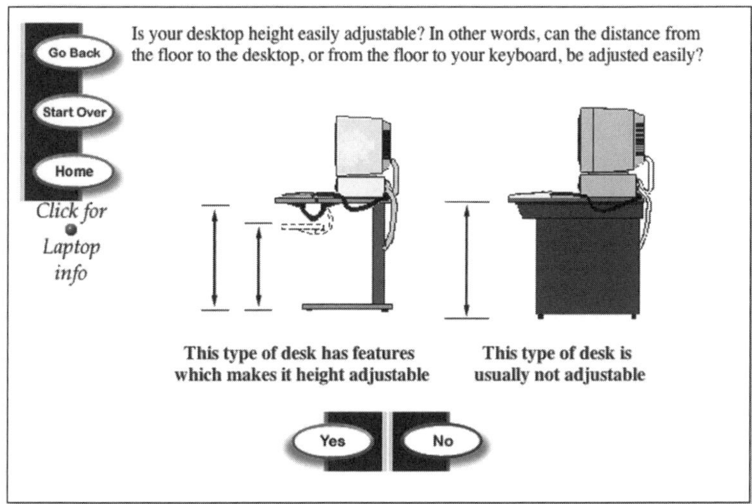

© Ergostar Ergonomic Adjustment Program by The Starfield Group, Inc. Reprined with permission.

FIGURE 6.1 The free online ergonomics adjustment program offered by Starfield Group, Inc., provides suggestions for simple, inexpensive adjustments that can make student and teacher workstations ergonomically sound.

You may not be able to purchase new furniture or invest in ergonomic peripherals, but you can still take steps to improve your work environment. For instance, when setting up your classroom, be aware of where windows and light fixtures are located and avoid placing computers in spots guaranteed to get monitor glare.

Adjustable chairs are often not an option in classrooms or labs, but you can provide simple footrests (even a backpack works) for students whose feet dangle when sitting in chairs that are too high. Alternatively, you can provide some type of booster seat (e.g., a thick cushion) for chairs that are too low.

Are the tables too low or too high? Ask the custodian to adjust them for you. It's also important to stress good posture and insist that students take breaks every 30 minutes or so. You can find a number of tips, articles, and other information for home and school at the Cornell University Ergonomics Web site (http://ergo.human.cornell.edu).

Use the following table to identify problems with workstations and to brainstorm some possible solutions.

TABLE 6.4 ■ **Performance Indicator VI.D.**

Promote safe and healthy use of technology resources.

Directions: Use the following checklist to identify potential ergonomic problems in your and your students' workstations in the classroom or lab.

1. Teacher workstation: Which of the following accommodations are in place?	Yes	No
Keyboard trays are adjustable and at a negative slope to avoid wrist and arm strain.		
The height and back support position of the workstation chair are adjustable.		
The workstation chair has pivotable, adjustable armrests.		
The mouse is placed on a tray or platform that can be positioned close to the body, above the keyboard.		
The monitor is positioned so that the top is 2 to 3 inches above the user's line of sight.		
The monitor is placed approximately one arm's length from the user.		
The monitor screen is free from glare.		
You take frequent breaks when using the computer workstation (every 30–60 minutes).		
What modifications need to be made in your workstation?		

2. Student workstations: Which of the following accommodations are in place?	Yes	No
Computer monitors are placed so that students don't strain their necks and eyes because they must look up to work.		
Monitor screens are free from glare.		
Keyboards are placed on a flat surface, at elbow level.		
The mouse is located right next to the keyboard.		
Students whose feet don't touch the floor when they're seated are encouraged to place a backpack on the floor, under their feet.		
Students take frequent breaks when using the computer workstation (every 30 minutes).		
What modifications need to be made for student workstations?		

(Continued)

TABLE 6.4 ■ **Performance Indicator VI.D.** *(Continued)*

3. Staff and student laptops: Which of the following accommodations are in place?	**Yes**	**No**
External keyboards are available to users.		
External mice are available to users.		
External monitors are available to users.		
Users are discouraged from placing laptops on high tables or desks.		
Users are discouraged from placing laptops on their laps.		
What modifications need to be made for laptop use?		
4. What specific steps will you take to improve workstations for yourself and your students?		

Ensuring Equitable Access to Technology Resources

Performance Indicator VI.E.

Facilitate equitable access to technology resources for all students.

Educators often use the student-to-multimedia-computer ratio as a yardstick for equal access to technology in schools. Nationally, this ratio is lower than ever before. According to Education Week's *Technology Counts 2005* report, the 2004 national ratio of students to multimedia computers used for instruction was 4.6:1. State ratios ranged from a low of 2:1 in South Dakota to a high of 6.9:1 in Nevada. But physical proximity to hardware is just one very small part of the whole equal access picture. Equity also depends on the usability of the available hardware and the kinds of technology-supported learning experiences students are afforded.

Basic Issues with "Stuff"

The Education Week report also looks at Internet connectivity in schools. Student access to Internet-based resources and tools is essential for effective use of technology. Ninety-nine percent of U.S. schools have Internet connections, but the national ratio of students to Internet-connected computers is considerably higher than the ratios reported above (see table 6.5). This means that far fewer students have opportunities to engage in technology-based experiences that capitalize on the potential of Internet use than you might think if you look only at overall ratios.

TABLE 6.5 ■ **Number of students per Internet-connected computer (2004)***

	Classrooms	Computer Labs	Library/Media Centers
Number of students	8:1	12.6:1	57:1

**As reported in Technology Counts 2005.*

Additional factors that may be glossed over, but which impact basic access, include the age, condition, and placement of equipment. No matter what an inventory sheet may say, students whose technology experiences are limited to vintage or unreliable equipment do not have the same access as students who get to work with newer, reliable equipment.

In many schools, new equipment is placed in labs, while older, less reliable equipment is rotated out to classrooms. Or, upper-grade classrooms receive the newest equipment and older computers are shifted to lower-grade classrooms. Unless they're part of a thin client network, vintage systems simply cannot run newer software or be used effectively for Web-based tools and resources. When you factor in the technical support issues that are par for the course with older equipment, you begin to see how these practices almost guarantee unequal access within a school.

The ongoing debate about placement of hardware in labs versus classrooms adds another dimension to this discussion of equal access. Thirty years ago, when computers were very expensive, difficult to move around, and new to most teachers, restricting technology access to labs made more sense. But things have changed. Prices have dropped dramatically. There's even an MIT project that promises fully functional $100 laptops for schools in the very near future. From laptops to handhelds, mobile technologies are increasingly popular instructional tools. Also increasingly, the majority of teachers have at least basic technology proficiency skills. Most important, according to a report by CDW Government, Inc. (2005), nearly two-thirds of the teachers surveyed stated they want more technology access in their classrooms.

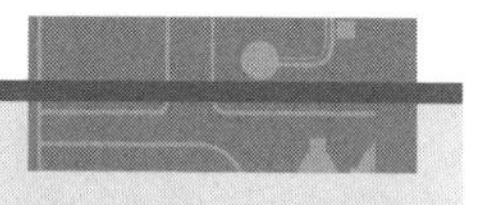

Thin Client Network

A thin client network can bring new life to old computers because the individual computers, or thin clients, have little or no installed software. Instead, software applications and files are stored on the network's server and accessed using the individual computers as workstations. This means that antiquated systems may be used to run newer programs.

Most experts recommend that schools strive to offer both labs and classroom computers so that teachers and students have access when it's needed, rather than when the schedule permits. Fixed and mobile labs do serve a purpose. It's easier to introduce new technology skills using a lab, particularly when the student to computer ratio is 1:1, and if there's access to a support person who can lend a helping hand. Labs are also useful when students need to work on individual assignments at the same time.

However, there are drawbacks, not the least of which is scheduling. Those "teachable moments" that could be significantly enhanced through a technology-supported activity or a quick check online don't always occur when it happens to be your turn to use the lab. Teachers who have daily access to at least four or five Internet-connected computers in their classrooms are better positioned to capitalize on these moments. They're also more likely to incorporate use of technology as one of many learning tools than their counterparts who don't have easy access.

What You Do with What You Have

Teachers and students can have physical access to up-to-date technology, but that's just the beginning. What a teacher does with the technology is what really matters. There are many schools where technology is readily available, but students aren't provided regular opportunities to use what's there. Students who were surveyed for the 2002 report *The Digital Disconnect* (Levin & Arafeh, 2002, August 14) said the majority of their education-related use of the Internet took place outside the school day. They also reported wide variations of technology use among their teachers, stating that few required it, some allowed it, and a small group actually forbade its use. This means that educators need to consider *how* available technologies are being used and what can be done to improve or enhance that use. Two factors that impede equitable access to quality technology-based instruction include

- lack of consistent expectations for *regular* use of various technologies, and
- lack of consistent expectations for *appropriate* use of various technologies.

Educators need to take a long, hard look at how use of technology is incorporated into daily classroom practice to ensure that students aren't being denied equitable access due to adult-imposed constraints.

It's obvious that students of teachers who avoid technology use at all costs are getting the short end of the stick. But there are more subtle access issues in classrooms where technology is used in limited ways. Chapter 2 (Performance Indicators II.A. and II.B.) includes a discussion of the Apple Classrooms of Tomorrow Project (1995), whose research identifies five stages of use of technology. Students in classrooms where teachers confine lesson design to the adoption or adaptation stages don't have the same kind of access as students whose teachers offer instructional experiences at the appropriation or invention stages of use.

In the first type of classroom, student use is generally restricted to learning skills, such as keyboarding and basic use of applications, or to using drill-and-practice software, usually for remediation. These students typically use technology to fill time. When their other work is done (or if they've been good), students are permitted to use a computer to play a game or type a paper that's been drafted by hand. While this level of use may appeal to some students, it has no impact on their academic achievement because they're not required to use critical-thinking or problem-solving skills to complete the task at hand. In the long run, most students are quickly bored with this kind of activity.

In the second type of classroom, technology use is not an add-on. All students, regardless of ability level or other challenges, have opportunities to use technology tools to work collaboratively to complete projects or solve real-world problems. These assignments are an integral part of the instructional day and challenge students to apply skills in meaningful ways. This doesn't mean that students engage in this kind of activity on a daily basis. There's a need to teach discrete skills. However, it does mean that throughout the school year, students should be offered opportunities to make meaning of their learning in significant ways.

Use the following table to identify possible equal-access issues in your own classroom and find solutions.

TABLE 6.6 ■ **Performance Indicator VI.E.**
Facilitate equitable access to technology resources for all students.

Directions: Give a Yes or No answer to the following questions. Use the short-answer areas to elaborate on your answers or respond to prompts.

1. Do you use technology access as a reward or punishment in your classroom?	Yes	No
Explain:		
2. Do students at all levels of academic ability have opportunities to use technology to increase problem-solving and critical-thinking skills in your classroom?	Yes	No
Explain:		
3. Are there technology access issues for your students who are in special education programs?	Yes	No
Explain:		
4. Are there technology access issues for your students based on gender?	Yes	No
Explain:		
Summarize the access issues in your classroom. List steps you will take to ensure equal access for all your students:		

Action Plan

Now that you've read about each performance indicator for Standard VI and have had the opportunity to think about your level of implementation for each indicator, it's time to develop an action plan to improve or expand your professional practice in this area.

First, review your responses to the statements and questions in each performance indicator table. It's not possible to master every indicator at once, so choose one at a time. Build your plan using the steps that you identified you might take for the chosen performance indicator and complete your action plan by using the table below. Performance Indicator VI.A. has been used as a sample.

TABLE 6.7 ■ **Teachers understand the social, ethical, legal, and human issues surrounding the use of technology in PK–12 schools and apply that understanding in practice**

Performance Indicator	Next Steps	I need to work on this step with the following people...	I will know this step has been achieved when...	Timeline
VI.A. Model and teach legal and ethical practice related to technology use.	*Develop and teach at least one lesson plan per semester to review the student AUP.*	*Grade-level team members, offering to share and work collaboratively with them.*	*The lesson plans are written and taught.*	*Sept. 15, Jan. 15*
	1.			
	2.			
	3.			

Resources

ARTICLES AND REPORTS

Apple Classrooms of Tomorrow Project. (1995). *ACOT's 10 year report.* [Online report]. Available: www.apple.com/education/k12/leadership/acot/library.html

CDW Government, Inc. (2005). *Teachers talk technology 2005.* [Online report]. Available: http://newsroom.cdwg.com/features/feature-08-29-05.htm

Education Week. (2005). *Technology Counts 2005.* Vol. 24, Issue 35. [Online report]. Available: www.edweek.org/ew/toc/2005/05/05/index.html

Future of Networking Technologies for Learning. *Copyright and K–12: Who pays in the network era?* [Online article]. Available: www.ed.gov/Technology/Futures/rothman.html

Levin, Douglas, & Arafeh, Sousan. (2002, August 14). *The digital disconnect.* [Online report]. Available: www.pewInternet.org/pdfs/PIP_Schools_Internet_Report.pdf

Reilly, R. *How to create a bad acceptable use policy document (and have it survive)!* [Online article]. Available: www.teachers.net/gazette/MAR02/reilly.html

Virginia Department of Education Division of Technology. *Acceptable use policies: A handbook.* [Online handbook]. Available: www.pen.k12.va.us/go/VDOE/Technology/AUP/home.shtml

TOOLS

Starfield Group, Inc. *ErgoStar software for public schools teaching grades K–12.* Available: www.ergostar.com/K-12.shtml

WEB SITES

Baltimore County Public Schools Office of Equity and Assurance. Available: www.bcps.org/offices/oea/publications/

Center for Assistive Technology & Environmental Access. Available: www.catea.org

Consortium for School Networking. *Cyber security for the digital district.* Available: www.securedistrict.org

Copyright with Cyberbee. Available: www.cyberbee.com/copyrt.html

Council for Exceptional Children. Available: www.ideapractices.org

Cornell University Ergonomics Website. Available: http://ergo.human.cornell.edu

Information Technology Services. *Computer ethics institute.* Available: www.brook.edu/ITS/CEI/CEI_HP.HTM

Keystone Central School District. *Fair use of copyright in the K–12 classroom.* Available: www.kcsd.k12.pa.us/technology/copyright/index.html

Oregon Occupational Safety and Health Division. *Computer ergonomics for elementary school.* Available: www.orosha.org/cergos/index.html

University at Buffalo, School of Public Health and Health Professions. *Assistive technology training online project.* Available: http://atto.buffalo.edu

Conclusion

I earned my first teaching credential in 1978. One course activity remains vivid in my memory nearly 30 years later. The instructor asked us to read and discuss H. R. W. Benjamin's *Saber-tooth Curriculum, Including Other Lectures in the History of Paleolithic Education*, published by McGraw-Hill in 1939. Although almost 70 years old, portions of this text are still relevant to today's educators. You can read an adaptation of the chapter I read as a student at http://nerds.unl.edu/pages/preser/sec/articles/sabertooth.html, but here's a quick summary.

> New Fist, an early Stone Age man, develops the first formal curriculum, devising lessons to teach their youngsters skills that will significantly improve the quality of their lives. Topics include fish-grabbing-with-bare-hands, wooly-horse-clubbing, and saber-tooth-tiger-scaring-with-fire. The curriculum is highly successful for many years.
>
> One day, a new ice age dawns. Muddy rivers make it impossible to see and grab fish. The wooly horses leave for a more desirable climate, and the saber-tooth tigers become extinct. Some members of the tribe suggest it's time to revise the curriculum and teach new skills more applicable to the changed environment. These skills include net-making, antelope-snaring, and bear-killing.
>
> But tribal leaders scorn their ideas. "If you had any education yourself," they say severely, "you would know that the essence of true education is timelessness. It is something that endures through changing conditions, like a solid rock standing squarely and firmly in the middle of a raging torrent. You must know that there are some eternal verities, and the saber-tooth curriculum is one of them!"

Educators are engaged in a similar debate today. One side argues that they already have a complete curriculum and that they're hard-pressed to cover it in the time allotted. This group tends to believe that what students need is a firmer foundation in the time-honored "fundamentals." Members of the opposing side point out that we live in times of rapid change. They take the position that up-to-date activities are needed to make education relevant for today's students. David Warlick states this position in an August 29, 2006, post on his Two Cents Worth blog (http://davidwarlick.com/2cents/). He writes:

> 1. Can a teacher be a good teacher without using technology? A resounding "YES!"
>
> 2. Is a teacher who is not using technology doing their job? An emphatic "NO!"

> If we can expand what it means to be literate to reflect the changing information environment, and integrate that, then we might start using technology for what it is, the pencil and paper of our time.

All too often, today's students are walking into classrooms where they're taught the modern equivalent of the saber-tooth curriculum. Technology use on many school campuses first occurred when a few determined teachers saw its potential as an instructional tool. This grassroots approach is no longer sufficient. Every student has the right to be taught in classrooms where teachers provide instruction that's firmly rooted in digital-age skills. Every educator must take responsibility for making this happen.

For some of you this means starting at the very beginning. You'll need to develop personal proficiency in the basic technology skills outlined in NETS•T Standard I. However, mastering basic skills such as word processing, using an electronic grade book, or searching the Internet is not enough. Simple technology proficiency doesn't make anyone a better teacher.

Becoming an effective digital-age educator will require you to look beyond basic proficiency to see the bigger picture. Essential skills are

- the ability to envision digital-age instruction and articulate that vision,
- knowledge of a variety of instructional practices,
- knowledge of the curriculum and content standards,
- knowledge of how to use data to make instructional decisions,
- a personal willingness to be a lifelong learner, and
- the ability and desire to regularly work collaboratively with colleagues.

If you possess these skills, you're able to work with colleagues, administrators, students, and parents to research, plan, implement, and evaluate instructional programs that capitalize on the capabilities of technology, resulting in increased student engagement and performance.

You must also have certain essential understandings to create an environment where technology is used as a tool for effective instruction. You must understand that

- your primary concern is student achievement;
- you must find an effective balance between teacher-directed and student-centered activities at whatever grade level you teach, K–12;
- instructional planning must be predicated upon analysis of appropriate data;
- instructional planning must be collaborative and dynamic;
- regular monitoring and evaluation of instruction must take place to continue to move forward;
- you must participate in regular, ongoing professional development opportunities in a variety of formats, both on and off site;

- you and your students must have ready access to up-to-date equipment that is reliable and well maintained;
- you must be knowledgeable about and address concerns regarding equal access; social, legal and ethical issues; and system security and use.

Successful digital-age teachers are willing to take the time to work collaboratively and leverage resources to create sustained commitment to instructional programs on this scale. Unfortunately, many teachers are disconnected from the world of instructional technology. This situation has various causes, but the fact of the matter is that whatever the reasons, if you haven't embraced classroom technology use by now, you need to do so. The purpose of the NETS•T is to help you become more effective by demystifying the role of technology in education.

Standards and performance indicators alone are not enough, however. You also need resources that will assist in implementing the standards. This book is one resource for teachers, school administrators, and institutions of higher learning to use as they begin working with the standards. In addition to the narratives explaining each performance indicator, the questions and statements that encourage reflective responses, and the action plan template, a wide range of additional resources are identified in each chapter. Additional ISTE publications may also be used. For example, *National Educational Technology Standards for Teachers: Resources for Student Assessment* provides tools and strategies for measuring teacher performance in meeting the standards.

Local situations will vary, and technology advances rapidly. This makes it difficult, if not impossible, to develop a definitive description of the ideal technology-using teacher. But by using the information and activities provided in this book within the context of your own situation, you'll become a more effective digital-age teacher.

One final suggestion for those of you who are working toward sustained use of instructional technology. Document and share the positive results of technology integration practices using measurable outcomes combined with human-interest narratives. This practice makes your efforts more comprehensible and real to members of the school community and the public. For example, it's helpful to know, based on ongoing assessment, that students' continuing retention of content material improves in classrooms where technology-based collaborative projects are introduced. When these data are coupled with a brief vignette describing one particular project, the impact of the assessment results becomes more powerful.

Sharing this kind of information takes many forms. For example, you can

- post aggregate assessment results and sample student projects on your classroom Web site,
- take examples of successful projects to grade-level, departmental, or general faculty meetings to display and discuss, or
- ask to use an office bulletin board to share lesson highlights with staff and members of the public.

Teachers are clamoring for examples of best practices in technology integration. A number of venues are available to those of you willing to share your experiences and the materials you've developed. For example, teachers are encouraged to submit proposals to speak at conferences, such as the one sponsored by ISTE (the National Educational Computer Conference) and those sponsored by ISTE affiliate organizations. Many online and print journals encourage teachers to contribute articles. Celebrate your successes by showcasing your work both online and in print.

In the process, you'll find a worldwide network of educators working toward the same goal: helping students prepare themselves to be self-sufficient, productive citizens in the digital age.